Life is a Buffet

Life is a Buffet

✦

So Save Room for Dessert

Polly D Boyette

iUniverse, Inc.

New York Lincoln Shanghai

Life is a Buffet
So Save Room for Dessert

iUniverse books may be ordered through booksellers or by contacting:

iUniverse
2021 Pine Lake Road, Suite 100
Lincoln, NE 68512
www.iuniverse.com
1-800-Authors (1-800-288-4677)

ISBN-13: 978-0-595-36797-9 (pbk)
ISBN-13: 978-0-595-81212-7 (ebk)
ISBN-10: 0-595-36797-6 (pbk)
ISBN-10: 0-595-81212-0 (ebk)

Printed in the United States of America

Contents

INTRODUCTION

In my family, I'm known as Polly D. The "D" is for my middle name, which is Deborah. Somehow or other my middle initial became part of my first name, probably because in the South it seems that everyone has to be called by more than just one name. My sister's name is Robin Lynn, but we call her Robbie Lee. I don't know exactly why, but we do. Robbie Lee and I share a home. We're both single and probably get along better than your average sisters, so living together just made good sense. We share expenses, clothes, and money. It all seems to work out fine, all in all, and we enjoy ourselves. A few years back our mother, AC, moved in with us too.

Now our mom's name breaks all Southern rules. She has no middle name. Heck, there's no first name either. It seems her mother and father ran slam out of names when they were raising their large family, and so they resorted to just picking random letters of the alphabet. The letters don't stand for anything at all; it's just "AC" Don't laugh. She has a twin brother named "JT," but we won't get into that. She's always getting mail addressed to Mr. AC or letters requesting that she please provide her full name and stop kidding around. But she's managed to live with it for years, so we don't make too big a fuss over it.

Mom was raised in Bagley, North Carolina, but spent most of her adult life living in Virginia. Robbie Lee and I are Virginia born and raised. However, we've mocked Mom's North Carolina accent so much that we now talk pretty much the same as she does, with a few exceptions. Mom has her own dialect, and she sometimes makes up words as she goes along. I grew up thinking "sink" was pronounced "zink." "Go put these dishes in the zink for me," Mom would say, or "I see'd and know'd that would happen." Over time we've come to learn the correct pronunciation for most words, but we sometimes still say them wrong for the pure joy of it.

Together, Robbie Lee, AC, and I have had some hilarious adventures that I've shared with many people throughout my lifetime. I learned to laugh at myself and my family long ago. What follows is a collection of short humorous anecdotes mixed in with some simple truths from the Bible.

Why the Bible Scriptures, you ask? As a Christian, I study Scripture for applications to my life and my Christian walk. I've often found there's humor in

1

God's Word as I think of it in reference to some of the funny things that have happened to my family. I'm embarrassed to admit these stories are true, but they are. Like the time my mother called me at work to ask if I was aware that I could catch a computer virus while working with a computer all day. No, I'm not making this up. She heard it on the news and wanted me to tell my boss that I could no longer use my computer until a cure for the virus was found. I was also instructed to call my sister and warn her. I selected some of these stories to illustrate (with tongue-in-cheek) how the Bible can be used for everyday application to the sometimes crazy and embarrassing moments in our lives.

After reading these, you may say to yourself, "This family is crazy," but rest assured we're not. We've just had a lot of funny things happen to us over the years, just as your family probably has. These incidents have become more than memories; they've actually become the more cherished parts of my family life. When I've shared these stories with friends, they've helped them see the lighter side of their families, and before you know it, we're spouting out one funny story after another, and sometimes laughing through the tears.

While you're laughing, perhaps you will also allow God's Word to minister to your heart. I'm a firm believer that God has a sense of humor. After all, He made us in His image, didn't He? I don't think He would have given us the ability to laugh if this fact weren't true. Perhaps the main purpose of this book is to encourage others to appreciate their families, even with all their annoying, stressful, demanding, and sometimes embarrassing characteristics. Life does offer us many choices. Even though we didn't get to choose our family, we can make the choice to find the lighter side of family life. You can choose laughter. Choose to laugh at the embarrassing moments or the annoying family members. I'm not saying life doesn't have its more serious sides at times. I lost a brother to cancer along the way. There was nothing funny about that time in my life. Yet I find myself now looking back at the life we had and choosing to remember the times we laughed together, or remembering, for instance, the time he fell into a cold mountain stream trying to demonstrate to the rest of us the best method of crossing over to the other side.

The point I'm trying to make with this book is that we can choose to dwell on the hard, negative, depressing parts of life, or we can choose to focus on the lighter side of family life and everyday living, and learn to laugh at ourselves and the situations we sometimes encounter. Will we cry sometimes? Yes, but choosing to find the time to laugh will carry us through those harder bumps in life. Life truly is a buffet, offering us many choices along the way. Make one of those choices laughter. You'll find it's contagious.

CONVERSATIONS WITH AC

Mom, or AC as she's known to others, came from a large family and lived on a farm in North Carolina during the Depression. When she was just a teenager, she suffered a near-fatal heart attack from some medication she had been given to slow down her naturally fast heart. The attack kept her in bed for almost two years. She even had to learn to walk all over again. Her daddy, Charlie, vowed that if she lived, he would never lay a hand on her to whip her or make her do anything she didn't want to do. Consequently, my mother was spoiled rotten by her father, who loyally kept his promise. While her siblings were out working in the tobacco and cotton fields, she would complain of being too hot or too tired, and immediately she would be relieved of her chores and sent back to the house. This didn't go over well with her brothers and sisters, but it worked over and over again nonetheless.

I tell you my mother's background because it still plays a part in her life. She moved in with Robbie Lee and myself years ago, after our father died, and I quickly learned she still lived under the same vows her father had made many years ago. She's very healthy for her age and is capable of doing many things. She often doesn't choose to take the initiative to do them, however. For example, when Robbie Lee and I would arrive home late from work some nights, our conversations would go something like this.

"I'm so glad you're both finally home. I'm about to starve to death."

"Mom, why didn't you cook something?"

"I didn't know you wanted me to cook."

"Well, you could see we weren't home from work yet. Why didn't you just start something yourself?"

"How was I supposed to know what you wanted to eat? I can't just walk in the kitchen and start cooking without knowing what you want me to fix."

"Why not? You cooked for us for years when we were growing up. Did you suddenly forget how to put a meal together?"

"Yeah, but I was out planting daffneydills all day today, and I just didn't think about it."

"They're called daffodils, Mom, not daffneydils, and now what are we supposed to do? It's too late for me to start cooking, and you know nobody wants to eat what Robbie Lee fixes."

"Well, why didn't you call me and tell me to fix supper?"

"Because I didn't know I was going to get stuck in traffic and be this late, and besides, why do I have to call you? Why can't you just look at the time and decide to start supper on your own?"

"Ya'll just expect me to walk in that kitchen and pull something out of thin air and fix it?"

"Thin air? There's a freezer full of food in there. You just select something and cook it."

"But what if it's not what you wanted? Then you'd be mad when you got home."

"I'd eat anything you fix. We love your cooking, Mom."

"Well, you didn't eat those brains and eggs I fixed the other night."

"*Nobody eats brains and eggs*! I mean just fix something normal."

"You see, that's what I mean. If I fixed brains and eggs you'd have fussed, and you fuss if I don't fix something. I see'd and know'd it'd be this way."

"Be what way, Mom?"

"I've been outside planting daffneydils all day and I'm just as tired as you are, but now you're fussing at me for not fixing supper."

"The yard is full of daffneydils, I mean daffodils, right now. What we need is supper, not flowers."

"I can't do anything right around here. But don't worry. Next year I'll probably be dead and you won't have to worry about me."

"Oh no, not the 'I'll probably be dead' speech."

"You want to get fried chicken from Hardee's?" asks Robbie Lee, who thinks fried chicken is the solution to all of life's problems.

"We might as well, 'cause I'm not cooking at this hour," I announce to nobody in particular.

So we change clothes and run up to Hardee's and bring back fried chicken, French fries, and coleslaw.

"Mom, come on. Let's eat before it gets cold!" I yell from the kitchen.

"I'm not eating," AC replies.

"What? Why not? I thought you were hungry."

"I'm not hungry. I'm just gonna lie on the couch and read my book."

"Fine, we'll just eat without you," I reply.

"Go ahead. Tomorrow I'll probably be dead anyway, so it don't make no difference whether I eat today or not."

Now you have to understand that Mom has been dying for as long as I can remember. She's as healthy as a horse, but she has been planning her funeral for nigh on fifty years now. She prefaces everything with, "If I'm not dead," or "I'll probably be dead," or "I feel like I'm dead." This is supposed to make Robbie Lee and me feel guilty. Sometimes it works.

(Several hours later)

"Here, Mom. We saved you a plate. Why don't you eat something? You don't want to get sick and die."

"Didn't you bring me no ice tea? You know I like ice tea with my chicken. Didn't you get biscuits with this? Did you eat them all? You know how I like biscuits with my chicken. It ain't fit to eat 'les there's biscuits on the plate."

And so it goes.

Mom loves flowers. She can carry on a conversation for days just about flowers. She eats, drinks, and sleeps flowers. Our yard is the envy of the neighborhood. She sometimes stands on the sidewalk in front of our house, pretending to sweep, just to be present to accept any compliments that might be paid by passing pedestrians. On Saturdays, Mom is usually dressed and waiting with her pocketbook on her arm and standing by the front door.

"What do ya'll have planned today?" AC asks.

"I thought I'd go up to the mall to see if I can find me something decent to wear. Why?" I ask already knowing the answer.

"Because I need to go and buy some peat moss for my flower beds. I also want to see if they have any pansies on sale."

"Well, we'll go there after we go to the mall."

"If we go later, all of the good peat moss will be gone."

"Mom, they always have peat moss. Besides, didn't we buy twenty bags last weekend?"

"I used it all up. Lordy, it takes a lot of peat moss to keep a garden looking like it should. You can't just grow flowers without having plenty of peat moss on hand. I've done without it all week."

"Mom, we live in a townhouse. How many bags of peat moss do you need?"

"I see'd and know'd it'd be this way if I asked to go to the nursery. I'll probably..."

"I know, you'll probably be dead next year and we won't have to buy any more peat moss. But you see, that's where you're wrong. We're going to bury you in peat moss, piles and piles of it."

"Polly D, just take her to the nursery for the peat moss so we can have some peace today. Otherwise we'll be listening to her go on all day long," suggests Robbie Lee. "But let's stop and get some fried chicken on the way."

"Yeah, that sounds good," agrees AC.

And that's how our Saturdays end up. No matter what season it is, we wind up at a nursery looking at flowers, peat moss, mulch, dirt, or bulbs for the next season. In between visits to the nursery, Mom reads to us all the newspaper ads that have anything to do with growing things. Over dinner she recites all the different types of flowers growing in our yard while I'm struggling to hear the evening news. Once a month she gets a letter that announces who won the yard of the month in the neighborhood. We then have to drive Mom over to see how in the world they could have possibly won. Unfortunately Mom has never won this award. She says it's because we live in a townhouse and do not have a proper size yard.

Mom is also famous for singing around the house. I like it because it makes me feel at home. Mom has been singing around the house for as long as I can remember. She very seldom sings the same song for very long. She jumps from song to song; sometimes right in the middle of a song she'll switch to a whole other tune. Mostly she sings hymns, but sometimes she throws a country tune in there, which can sound kind of strange. Once when I was sitting in the living room and she was singing away in the kitchen, I thought I heard her singing, "Softly and tenderly, Jesus is calling, calling for you and for me. Put your sweet lips a little closer to the phone." I had to stop and think for a minute. "That's not quite right, is it?" Mom just continued singing, switching back and forth between the two songs, never missing a beat.

Mom doesn't have a lot of interests outside of flowers, country music, and romance novels. When she's on the couch in the evening, she has a romance novel in her hands. The whole house could burn down around her, and she wouldn't even blink. I have come and gone from the house without seeing her move a muscle for hours, other than to turn the pages of her book. Once while she was reading, Maggie, our sheepdog, ate the entire contents of a huge Easter basket close by. Pots have boiled over, meat has burned, and biscuits have cooked beyond recognition while AC has read her romance novels. Even though she is totally oblivious to everything around her while she's reading, she'll finally put the book down after hours have passed and say, "You know, ya'll hardly ever talk to me." Even though I could have accidentally amputated my leg and hopped on one foot around her on the couch, she'd never notice. But now she wants to know why we never talk to her.

"OK, let's talk," I say.

Robbie Lee just moans in the background.

"Did you know that George Clooney didn't like making Batman?" AC asks.

"No, I didn't."

"He said he was so tired when he got home from filming that he didn't have the energy to do anything else."

"Oh."

"That's how I feel sometimes."

"Uh-huh."

"Sometimes I feel like I'll be dead before morning."

"Uh-huh."

"Did you know that when I die I want a closed coffin?"

"Why?"

"I don't want people parading by me criticizing my hair, and how I look before they stuff me away in the ground."

"Mom, people like to pay their last respects. Can't we talk about something else?"

"Did you know Wal-Mart has daffneydils on sale for $1.99 a six-pack? Is that a good price?"

"I don't know."

"Why don't you?"

"I just don't. That's all. I have no idea what daffneydils, I mean daffodils, should cost."

"I want to get some this weekend if they look decent."

"Right."

Robbie Lee moans some more.

"What would happen if the astronauts went to the moon when it was only a half-moon?"

"Huh?"

"What if they started to land and it was only half a moon?"

This question I don't even try to answer. I just give her one of my infamous blank stares.

"Did you like George Clooney's hair in his last movie?"

"I don't know."

"I thought it looked terrible. Didn't you, Robbie Lee?"

More groans.

"I think he looks better with it longer. Don't you?"

"Whatever."

And so the conversation goes until Robbie Lee and I can't take any more and go to bed. Mom, picking up her romance novel, heads off to bed with her grumpy fifteen year old white dog, Jasper. As she closes the door to her room I have to pause and listen as she cheerfully sings to her dog, "Jasper the Jasper. I love you, Jasper. Jasper, Jasper. I love you." Shaking my head, I mumble to myself, "Good God," and turn off the lights.

COLOSSIANS 1:11
"Being Strengthened With All Power According To His Glorious Might
So That You May Have Great Endurance And Patience."

Sometimes patience and endurance are very hard to muster up. It's the little things in life that can cause us to blow our tops or reduce us to mere grunts and groans. Oh, we can handle the big deals in life without wincing, but leave us alone in a room with our mothers, and we twist ourselves into tight little knots we can't undo. We get wound so tight that we spin out of control like a tornado destroying everything in our path, or we shrink back into the ground like a withered plant.

Sometimes conversations with my mother can do that to me. I find myself able to handle most things in life, but I stumble through the simplest talks with her. It takes a great deal of patience on my part, along with great endurance. After all, she's elderly, and we have different interests.

I vow not to lose my patience, but over and over again I find myself failing. Every morning I pray, "Lord, please give me the patience I need; the patience my mother had with me while she managed to run a home with four children underfoot."

I think of the patience she had while she shopped with me pulling on her hand and screaming at the top of my lungs. I remember the endurance she displayed so bravely while she waited for us to grow from runny-nosed children into impatient adults. Then every night I repent because I didn't quite meet my goal that day. No matter what our test may be, God can provide the strength, patience, and endurance we need to deal with all of life's experiences, whether big or small.

JUST GOING HOME FROM THE BEACH

Robbie Lee and I were driving home after spending all day enjoying the sand and the beautiful ocean in the city of Virginia Beach. We were both wearing big floppy hats, huge T-shirts with beach scenes on them, baggy shorts, and flip-flops. We had been swimming, so our hair was neatly matted to the top of our heads—thus the hats.

On the way, I decided I was hungry. "Let's stop and get some take-out."

"All right, how about Moseberth's Fried Chicken? It's always good," replied Robbie Lee.

"No, I was thinking more like a sandwich or something light."

"But I'm really hungry. I don't think a sandwich will do it for me," Robbie Lee said, rubbing her belly.

"Look, there's a place," I said pointing to a little restaurant by the side of the road. "Let's go in and see what they have. It looks like a deli, so they probably have a little bit of everything."

As we pulled in, we noticed there were lots of cars in the parking lot.

"Boy, there sure are a lot of people here. I don't know if I want to go in dressed like this," said Robbie Lee, pulling down the sun visor's mirror. "I'm a real sight."

"Oh, we'll just rush in and get something to go," I said, not even bothering to look in the mirror.

Upon entering the deli, we could smell fried chicken. Robbie Lee spotted the buffet right away and ran over to see what was in it. I casually strolled over to the counter to look at the sandwich menu.

"Hey Polly D, they have fried chicken, mashed potatoes, and lots of hot vege-tables over here. It looks great."

"I want to see what kind of sandwiches they have first," I yelled back.

Suddenly a woman appeared behind the counter and in a low whisper asked, "May I help you?"

"Oh yes, I'm just trying to decide what kind of sandwich I want," I said, still studying the menu.

Robbie Lee yelled back with a huge grin on her face, "I know I'm getting fried chicken. Ask her how much the buffet would be to go."

The woman's eyes were following my floppy hat as I turned back and forth to carry on discussions with Robbie Lee across the room.

"Please excuse me…" started the woman behind the counter.

"Oh, just one more minute, please. You have so many choices," I said.

"Did you ask her how much the buffet is yet? These pieces of fried chicken are huge. Are you sure you don't want to get the buffet instead of a sandwich? Maybe we should call Mom and ask her if she wants us to bring her a plate too," said Robbie Lee, lustfully leaning over the steaming food.

"No, I'm sure she would much rather just have a sandwich."

"I'm sorry to interrupt you," the woman said in a quiet, polite voice, "but you see, we're closed."

"Closed?" I asked in utter shock. "How can you be closed? There are a hundred cars in the parking lot."

"You see, we're closed because we're hosting a private banquet." She pointed behind me to a table of well-dressed people all seated around a long table. Upon second glance, I noticed a speaker standing behind a podium. No one was speaking. In fact, everyone was just sitting and staring at us.

There wasn't a sound in the restaurant, except for the lone voice of Robbie Lee, "I'm going to get pork chops and fried chicken. Don't you want fried chicken, Polly D? It really looks good."

I snapped my head toward Robbie Lee and began to frantically motion for her to be quiet and to follow me.

"What are you doing? Aren't you going to get something to eat?"

"Come on," I said in a loud whisper, while the people at the table talked amongst themselves.

"But Polly D, why do we have to go somewhere else with all of this food here?"

"Just shut up and come on," I sputtered, heading toward the door.

Robbie Lee flip-flopped back toward me, and then we both quickly marched back to the exit.

"What's going on?" Robbie Lee still asked with her hands on her hips.

The woman behind the counter and the people at the table watched as I paused in my sprint toward the exit long enough to whisper in Robbie Lee's ear. Suddenly she let out a squeal like a pig caught in a barbed wire fence, while we bolted for the exit to the sound of our flip-flops on the recently waxed floor. We didn't stop running until we reached the car.

"I'm never coming back here again!" I cried.

"I don't know, they had a pretty good-looking buffet," laughed Robbie Lee. The car spun off around the corner toward home.

Later that evening, Robbie Lee, AC, and I enjoyed peanut butter and jelly sandwiches with cold glasses of milk and swore to never leave the house again.

Psalms 34:5

"Those who look to him are radiant; their faces are never covered with shame."

Ever have one of those embarrassing moments when you want to hide your head in a bag? I've had so many I can't begin to count them all, but they've certainly made life interesting. Sometimes we do things that would embarrass us to no end if anyone ever found out. We don't want anyone to think we're totally insane. Fitting in and feeling like part of the group is so important to us, yet something will always happen to make us stick out like a sore thumb.

I've learned to laugh at myself. If I hadn't, I wouldn't be able to show my face with some of the crazy things I've managed to do over the years. Fortunately, the Lord is never ashamed of us. He loves us no matter what. Where else can you find this kind of unconditional love? Even when we look our worst, or want to move to another state because of something we've done, He still loves us as His very own child. Isn't it great to know that even in your most awkward moment, when everyone else is staring at you with their mouths hanging open, He's looking down at you with a great big smile? He'll help you get back up and keep on walking with your head held high. Learn to laugh at yourself. Stop taking everything so seriously.

EATING IN THE PRESENCE OF ENEMIES

There's nothing I enjoy more than going out to dinner at one of my favorite restaurants. There's one in Portsmouth, VA, where I used to live, named the Circle. The food there is absolutely the best. They have a great variety of selections and everything tastes like home cooking. On Sundays, they have the best buffet in town. You can get anything from roast beef to, of course my favorite, fried chicken. There's usually a line, but it's well worth the wait.

One particular Sunday afternoon we decided to stop at the Circle for the buffet. Robbie Lee and I waited patiently in line along with the other hungry guests for about fifteen minutes before we were finally shown to our table. The front of the restaurant is actually shaped in a somewhat circular fashion, with the tables lined up beside one another in front of a huge window. This is the only thing I don't really like about the restaurant. The tables are too close to each other. You actually feel like you have to join in on the other party's conversation because you can hear every word. You're practically sitting in their laps, but I endure this inconvenience because the food is so good.

Once we told the waitress we were having buffet, we were off and running to the goodies. I skipped right past the salads and made my way to the main dishes, like fish, chicken livers, roast beef, fried chicken, and the best stewed tomatoes I had ever put in my mouth. I filled up my plate quickly because I was about to pass out from starvation. I headed back to my table, leaving Robbie Lee still pouring over the salads.

I smiled at the people seated at the table next to ours as I passed them. They were already eating, and they gave me just a quick and polite half smile. You know, the kind that people flash at you when they have no idea who you are and the smile fades almost before you have a chance to see it. Anyway, I turned quickly to sit down, and once seated I couldn't believe my eyes. The people at whom I had just smiled and who had been casually eating their dinner now had glasses, plates, and food turned upside down on them and all across the once-white tablecloth. I thought to myself, *I wonder what could have happened to their table in such a short time. They looked fine when I smiled at them earlier, but now their whole table is in a disaster."* Then I noticed that they were glaring at me. *Why are they staring at me with such indignation? I didn't do anything."* Suddenly it dawned on me. My pocketbook had a long strap on it and apparently as I swung around to sit down my pocketbook swung across their table, destroying everything in sight.

"I'm so sorry. Please, let me help you clean up," I cried. My face felt like it was about to explode from embarrassment. Everyone was staring now. "I'll be glad to pay for any dry-cleaning bills you might have."

"Please, just leave us alone. We'll take care of everything," one of the ladies replied.

I took my seat again, but I didn't know what to do with myself. After all, they were seated right next to me. Of course, Robbie Lee was still lingering up at the buffet table, chatting with someone, not knowing that her sister was causing enough chaos to get us thrown out on our heads.

"I wish she'd hurry up and come back to the table so I won't have to endure this embarrassment alone," I whispered under my breath. But Robbie Lee continued to linger over the food, chatting away.

"Are you sure there's nothing more I can do for you?" I pleaded, wanting them to let me do something to make up for the mess I had made.

"No, please. Just leave us alone," the woman again requested, looking at me like she wanted to knock me down in the middle of the room and beat me to a bloody pulp. I decided it would be best to leave her be.

I tried to begin eating, but it was so difficult with the whole restaurant staring and pointing. Finally, Robbie Lee came and sat down in front of me.

"Hey, what happened to them? Was there a tornado or something?" Robbie Lee said loudly.

The people at the next table just glared in my direction.

"Shhhh! I did that. I destroyed their entire table with my pocketbook. I'm so humiliated."

"You did it? Oh, no. Can we do anything to help you?" Robbie Lee blurted out to the woman who had already given me a threatening look when I asked that.

"Robbie Lee, be quiet! They don't want our help. Let's just eat and get out of here, please," I said, hiding my face with my hands.

We both tried to eat, but it felt like the whole world was watching us.

"Your face is really red," Robbie Lee pointed out.

"Thank-you, but I realize my face is very red because it feels like it's on fire. Can we talk about something else, please?"

"OK, guess who I ran into waiting in the buffet line?" Robbie Lee asked, quickly changing the subject.

"Who?"

"Sherry. You remember her. I went to high school with her. She was telling me she's married now, and they live in Longwood Homes."

"Longwood Homes?" I said louder than I meant to. "Who'd she marry, a millionaire?" I asked, laughing out loud.

Now Robbie Lee's face was beet-red. "No," she said in a hushed tone. "She married the man sitting right next to you."

As Robbie Lee pointed at the man right beside me, who was now staring at me even harder, I tried my best to sink underneath the table. I wished the napkin had been bigger so I could have covered myself up in it and just disappear from sight, but I couldn't. I tried not to catch his eyes as I shoveled food into my mouth to keep me quiet.

But then something terrible happened. Robbie Lee got the giggles, and she passed them along to me. Every time we looked at each other, we would just lose it. The people next to us were getting madder and madder because they thought we were laughing at them. I kept trying to explain in between our bursts of laughter that we weren't actually laughing at them, but they weren't buying it. Robbie Lee and I finally gave up, asked for our checks, and left. We screamed in laughter all the way home. I was so humiliated, but at the same time, the whole thing was so comical.

If nothing else, I sure learned a lesson from that experience. Now when I go out to dinner, I always carry just a small purse in my hand, make no sudden moves, and never look other people in the eye.

PSALM 23:5
"You Prepare A Table Before Me In The Presence Of My Enemies."

An enemy is someone who is proposing or seeking to inflict injury on another, according to *Webster's Handy College Dictionary.* Do you have enemies? Well, maybe they're not people who want to actually injure you physically, but sometimes our enemies are disguised as friends. I use the term "friends" loosely here. They are actually posing as friends in order to find out all of the dirt in your life so that they can be the first to share it with others, or they want to be on the inside so they can throw roadblocks in your path to prevent your success. Know anyone like that in your life? Well, God sees the heart of each person, and He knows their true intentions.

Have you ever wanted to take matters into your own hands, and take revenge on someone who is making your life difficult? You know, God can actually use our enemies to complete His plan for our life. Your enemies may not realize it, but they could be doing exactly what God has allowed them to do. While we're plotting their demise, God is perhaps trying to build character into our lives by using this unreasonable person or He may turn to good what your so-called friend intended for harm.

Whatever the situation, God is always in control and will work things for the good of those who love Him. He provides us with protection and power against our enemy. He allows us to walk in safety and security, knowing that He is guiding our steps and that He alone holds the reins to our future and no one else. Rest in His peace and strength. Leave the unfair and untrue accusations for God to handle. You don't have to defend yourself against these things. God will contend with those who contend with you. In Romans 12:19–21 it says "Do not take revenge, my friends, but leave room for God's wrath, for it is written: 'It is mine to avenge. I will repay,' says the Lord. On the contrary: If your enemy is hungry, feed him; if he is thirsty, give him something to drink. In doing this, you will heap burning coals on his head. Do not be overcome by evil, but overcome evil with good."

WHAT BUS?

It was a sunny Monday morning as I started out for work. I found myself in an unusually good mood, considering it was a Monday. As I started my car, I noticed the windshield was wet from the morning dew. It made it particularly difficult to see when the sunlight hit the windshield so I turned on the window defroster to see if it would help. After deciding the window was as good as it was going to get, I headed down the road, making my way out to the busy commute to work. I tuned the radio to my favorite station and relaxed for a routine drive.

Suddenly, as I rounded a curve, the sun hit my wet windshield, and for a split second I couldn't see a thing. Hoping that within the next second I would drive out of the momentary blind spot, I kept on going. As it turns out, I was right. Just as quickly as the blind spot appeared, it disappeared. But there in the clearing, was the huge front end of a giant vehicle right in front of me. There was nowhere to go, so I slammed on brakes and braced myself for an unavoidable collision.

Crash! Bam! Boom! We collided and my head rocked back and forth until I thought it would snap right off my neck. My eyes rolled around in their sockets like I was one of those cartoon characters on TV. When I was finally able to focus, all I could see was the front end of a huge vehicle, right in the middle of my windshield.

"Oh, no!" I said to myself. "I've hit a garbage truck!"

But as I got out of the car, I could see that it wasn't a garbage truck, but a full-size school bus. There were people coming out of their houses from every direction up and down the street. I just stood by the car and prayed for calmness. Several people ran up to me and asked if I was all right, because the front of my car was completely smashed in.

"I believe I'm OK," I mumbled as I stared in disbelief at the huge school bus connected to the front of my small car.

"What happened?" someone asked me.

"I don't know. The sun hit my windshield and the next thing I knew, I'm wearing a school bus."

"Yeah, the sun's a real problem about this time of the morning through here," a bystander pointed out. "They should try to do something about it."

For a brief moment, I took my eyes off of the school bus just long enough to catch a glimpse of the clever person who was suggesting something be done about the sun. Funny, he didn't look that stupid, but I guess he was just trying to be helpful. But gradually my eyes returned to the vision of the long, yellow school bus in front of me.

"Maybe something should be done about the sun," I found myself saying.

In just a matter of minutes, the tiny little residential street was filled with chaos. The police arrived, along with a fire truck, another school bus, and a van carrying little women dressed in white. I guessed they were nurses. As I stepped a little closer to the bus, I looked inside and saw frightened children sitting inside.

"Oh, please, dear Lord, don't let anyone be hurt," I mumbled to myself as I examined their scared faces. Suddenly an officer tapped me on the shoulder and started to question me about the accident. I calmly explained what happened, feeling a little embarrassed when I came to the part about not seeing the bus.

"I know," said the officer. "I had to pull my squad car right behind you with my lights flashing so no one would run into your car. I almost didn't see it myself when I came around the corner. The sun is blinding right there."

I couldn't believe it. I wasn't losing my mind and eyesight after all. There really was a blind spot there in the road. I stood quietly and watched as they began transferring the children off of the bus onto another one. They held hands as they paraded past me. I realized as they slowly walked by that these were special education children. Not only did I hit a giant yellow school bus, but I hit one carrying special education children. They all glared at me as they passed.

"Is that the lady that hit us?" one small girl asked.

"Is she blind or something?" another asked.

"Why did you run over us, lady?" still another asked.

I just stayed calm and smiled as they made their way onto the other bus. How could I get into so much trouble only a half-mile from my house? I was in such a good mood that morning. I guess that'll teach me to wake up feeling happy on a Monday.

The officers finished their questions to me and the bus driver. No tickets were given out. They decided it was just a freak accident. As I watched my car being towed away, a gentleman in a trench coat from the school introduced himself to me.

"You know, ma'am, you look unusually calm to have just hit a school bus," he said in a suspicious voice.

"Yeah, I know. I prayed for calmness right from the beginning. I wish I had prayed not to hit a school bus before I left the house."

"Would you like me to give you a lift back home?" he kindly asked.

"No, thank you. I believe I'll just stroll on back home and call my work. I think today is one of those days I had better just play it safe and stay in bed."

I walked slowly back to my house. Neighbors who had waved good-bye to me as I drove off to work were now filled with curiosity as to why I was walking back home without my car. One minute I'm driving and the next I'm walking.

As I settled into bed with an aspirin for my aching head, I couldn't stop thinking about those special children staring at me as they marched past. It probably took the rest of the day for someone to explain to them how a grown woman could not see their school bus.

When Robbie Lee arrived home from work, she was very helpful and supportive. "A school bus? You hit a whole school bus? How could you not see a school bus? Aren't they big, yellow things? You didn't see it? Is it time to have your eyes examined? Wow, a whole school bus. I never in my life heard of such a thing. I've heard of night blindness, but not morning blindness."

I just pulled the covers up over my head and closed my eyes, vowing never to step foot out of bed as long as the sun was shining.

JOHN 9:25
"I Was Blind, But Now I See."

There are times when we don't have all of the pieces to the big picture, and we slam right into the unexpected. It's usually right at the time we think we have life on a string, and things seem to be going our way. Maybe we get cocky and careless. We forget to look both ways, or to pay closer attention, or to pray or read our Bibles. We fail to heed the warning signs, and, the next thing we know, we've been hit head-on by an unidentified flying object.

Never let yourself get to a place in your life where you think you have all the answers, or that you're too good to take the wise counsel of a godly friend. If you become too comfortable in your lifestyle and become lazy or too relaxed to pay needed attention to spiritual details, you may find yourself heading down the wrong track. And before you realize it, you've come face to face with something too big for you to get around. You can be stopped dead in your tracks while running on the fast lane. Don't let it happen to you. Take the time to read the Word and to find some quiet time with God. Nurture your spiritual life so when the time comes, you'll recognize the warning signs. Then instead of crashing directly into trouble, you'll be guided by the Holy Spirit around those obstructions in the roadway. You'll have a clearer vision of where you're going and the best way to get there.

POLLY D ADDS OIL TO HER CAR

As I started up the engine to my brown Mustang, I noticed the oil light came on and stayed on while the car was running. Checking my trusty owner's manual, I discovered the light was telling me I was low on oil, and I should add some immediately. So I drove up to the nearest grocery store, went in, and bought four quarts of oil. Not knowing anything about adding oil to an engine, I just popped the top off all of the bottles and poured all four quarts in, one after the other. I didn't bother stopping in between the quarts to check the oil level in the car. No, sir, I just poured until there was no more oil left to pour.

"There," I thought to myself. "That's done."

I felt very good that I had acted immediately to solve my problem. I disposed of the oil bottles and cranked up my car. The oil light came on again. As a matter of fact, it looked even brighter now.

It must be stuck, I thought. I slapped the dashboard a couple of times with my hand, hoping to jar something loose, but it didn't work. *Oh, well. At least I know it has plenty of oil in it now. It's bound to be all right to drive it.*

So I set out on my errands, not noticing that when I accelerated the gas, great mounds of white smoke were trailing my car. While I was sitting at a red light, I noticed smoke was beginning to encircle my car.

What in the world is that?" I wondered. *Somebody must need a new exhaust pipe.*

As I pushed the gas pedal to head through the green light, I looked in my rear-view mirror and realized that I couldn't see anything. It looked like I was driving in a huge cloud. The cars behind me were pulling off the road to get away from me. *Oh, no, it's me. I'm the one making all of the smoke.* I wondered if it had anything to do with the four quarts of oil I had just put in my car.

I immediately pulled off the road and into a grocery store parking lot and sat there for a moment, not really knowing what to do. Finally I decided it would be best to just take the car home and maybe call a mechanic and describe the problem over the phone. Just as I was about to pull away, an elderly woman was coming out of the store carrying two bags of groceries. She made the mistake of walking behind my car just as I was leaving. As the white smoke encircled her frail body, I prayed she would survive the exhaust. I kept trying to look through my mirror to see if I could see her, but the smoke was too thick. I just stepped on the gas and kept on going.

Once I arrived home, my neighbor came out of the house, waving his arms.

"What's going on with your car?" he asked. "I could see a trail of smoke following you all the way down the road."

"I'm not sure, but I'm about to call a mechanic," I replied, still worried that I might have just killed the old woman at the grocery store.

"Has anybody added oil to your car lately?" the neighbor asked.

"Uh, yeah, very recently," I answered.

"Well, you tell the dummy that he put too much oil in your car. That's what's causing it to smoke like this."

"Oh, yeah, I'll tell him," I replied, not wanting to admit that the dummy was me.

"I don't know how some of those idiots are allowed to work on people's cars. Anybody should know that you have to check, between adding quarts of oil to your car, to make sure you're not adding too much," he pointed out.

"Yeah, check in between, anybody would know that," I stuttered.

I hung my head and went inside to call the garage while my neighbor called people over to show them what someone had done to my car. I kind of confessed to the garage mechanic what really happened, but I never mentioned that I had made the mistake.

"Yeah, there are some idiots out there who think they know all about cars. You just bring in your car to us, ma'am, and we'll fix what the dummy did."

"Thank-you ever so much," I responded in my best Southern accent.

As I took the car in to have some of the oil drained from my engine, I felt as though I was driving through the Red Sea. Cars were parting on my left and my right all the way. Once there, I had to listen to still another speech about how stupid people shouldn't be allowed to work on cars. I just sat quietly and read the newspaper, nodding when it was appropriate and grunting in agreement now and then.

PSALM 23:5
"You Anoint My Head With Oil; My Cup Overflows."

Have you ever had too much of a good thing, or for that matter, a bad thing? It seems these days everything is done in excess, like eating, drinking, sex, and television, just to name a few. Moderation seems to be a word of the past. If some trend catches on, people go crazy with it until, finally, everyone grows tired of it and moves on to the next craze.

Sometimes our eyes are bigger than our stomachs, so to speak, and we think we have to have more than what's really needed. We always feel like we need more. Then one day we wake to find we have an excess of useless things that have to be discarded, or we've overspent big time and end up bankrupt.

Even though our material lives reflect excess, or at least a desire for excess, we often leave our spiritual lives lacking. We walk around empty, neglecting our spiritual needs while we're busy trying to fill up the gaps with more and more things. David says in Psalm 23, "The Lord is my shepherd, I shall not be in want." If we put the Kingdom of God first in our lives, He will take care of our needs and our desires. With God first in our life, everything else falls into its proper perspective. Then instead of having an excess of one thing polluting our hearts and minds, we find we have everything we need in Him. Trust Him to know what you need. His measuring stick is far better than ours.

FIRE, THERE'S A FIRE!

A friend of mine at work was telling us how her husband deep-fries turkeys for Thanksgiving and gives them away as gifts. The more she described how good it tasted, the more my mouth watered. I pulled her aside later and asked for all of the details so I could try it at home.

"You have to have a really big pot and a lot of cooking oil," she explained.

"Uh-huh," I answered as I wrote down every word she spoke.

"Here's a sample package of the marinade that you put inside of the syringe and shoot inside of the turkey. Then deep-fry it at 350 degrees for about three minutes for every pound the turkey weighs."

"Can you use this recipe to deep-fry a chicken instead of a turkey?

"Sure, I don't see why not.

"Uh-huh, uh-huh," I answered again, scribbling with great excitement.

"But most of all, you have to promise me that you will cook this chicken outside and not in your kitchen. The oil gets very hot and it's very dangerous to do this in your house. Do you have an outside cooker that you can use?"

"Uh-huh," I responded without really paying much attention. My mind was set on trying this delicious-sounding meal as soon as I got home.

"Now my husband usually does the cooking outside using special equipment designed for just such a purpose. If you don't know what you're doing, it can be very dangerous. Do you understand?" she asked.

"Uh-huh, I've got it. I'll be very careful. Thanks for all of the information," I shouted over my shoulder as I headed back to my desk.

As soon as I got home that night I yelled for Robbie Lee to come and help me in the kitchen, "Robbie Lee, we're going to cook up a delicious fried chicken tonight that will make your mouth think it's died and gone to heaven."

"Fried chicken? I love fried chicken," said Robbie Lee with great delight. It's her very favorite meal.

"Not just fried chicken. We're gonna deep-fry a whole chicken in just fifteen minutes."

"How're you gonna do that? Do you have what you need to deep-fry a whole chicken? Don't you have to have special equipment for that?" Robbie Lee asked with great worry in her voice.

"Nonsense, it's easy. All I need is a very big pot and a lot of oil. I stopped at the store on the way home and bought the chicken, oil, and a thermometer. We're all set. We have everything we need to cook this bird up just right. I can hardly wait to taste it."

"All right, I'm not the cook in the family. I guess you know what you're doing," said Robbie Lee. "What do you want me to do?"

"First pour those bottles of cooking oil into that pot I have on the stove. Then turn on the burner. I'll be preparing the chicken with this special marinade a friend gave me from work."

"But do you think this pot will be big enough? It doesn't look like it's gonna hold that chicken very well."

"Ah, it'll be fine. Besides, it's the biggest pot we have. Go ahead and fill it with oil. I'm sure it'll work OK," I said with great confidence. I was so eager to try the recipe that I didn't want to be bothered worrying about whether or not the pot was big enough.

"Shouldn't we be doing this outside?" Robbie Lee asked. "This is a lot of oil."

"We don't have a way to cook it outside. Just be careful, nothing will happen."

Robbie Lee poured all of the bottles of oil into the pot while I washed and shot the marinade into the chicken. I could almost taste it before we started cooking it.

"Imagine, in just fifteen minutes, we'll have a whole chicken fried up, ready to eat," I said.

I stuck the thermometer in the pot and began monitoring the temperature, waiting for it to reach 350 degrees. I had wired up the chicken with a makeshift handle so I could easily lower it into the pot. When the temperature was finally hot enough, I grabbed the chicken, which was dripping with the marinade, and dangled it over the pot. The oil began to bubble up from the drippings, so I sat the chicken back down for a moment.

"I think we have too much oil in here," I cleverly pointed out. "Maybe I'd better take some of it out."

With a heatproof glass cup I began dipping hot, hot oil out of the pot and into a glass baking dish. When I had lowered the amount of oil sufficiently, I again grabbed the chicken and lowered it into the pot. Suddenly, the oil came alive and started rising out of the pot. It spilled up and over the rim, until the burner underneath caught on fire.

"Oh my!" I screamed. "Robbie Lee, quick, come and help me. We've got to save the chicken."

I'm ashamed to admit that my first thoughts were for saving the chicken, but I was very hungry at the time. Robbie Lee ran around in circles while I finally got up the nerve to jerk the chicken out of the pot, slinging it all around the kitchen while I looked for a place to put it down. Hot oil was being splattered all over the walls and the floor. Robbie Lee was still running around in circles. The fire under the pot had grown bigger and looked very threatening.

"I'm going to call 911!" screamed Robbie Lee as she finally broke out of her circle and into the living room.

"Wait! Hand me the salt. Salt puts out grease fires."

Robbie Lee ran back into the kitchen, but when she hit the oily floor, she slid halfway across the room. I grabbed her just in time to keep her from falling, and we both danced around for a minute or two. In the meantime, the flames were growing bigger. Robbie Lee finally managed to get her balance and reached for the salt box. I was busy fanning and blowing on the flames, which made them grow even higher.

"Here, try this," Robbie Lee said, handing me the box of salt.

I threw salt on everything I could see, but the flames were underneath the pot and I couldn't get enough salt under there to smother the fire.

"I'm gonna have to move this pot so we can get salt under there," I shouted.

"No, let's just call 911," pleaded Robbie Lee. "You might drop the pot or it might catch on fire."

"I can do this," I announced bravely. "When I count to three, I'll pick up the pot and move it away from the burner. Then you start dumping salt on the fire. Ready?"

"All right," Robbie Lee said, holding the salt in her hand.

"One, two, three!" I picked up the pot with oil boiling over the sides and moved it away from the fire as my feet were slipping and sliding in different directions on the oily floor. Robbie Lee dumped the whole box of salt on the fire while screaming at the top of her lungs.

At last the fire was out. The kitchen was filled with smoke, soot, and oil as far as the eye could see. Robbie Lee and I sat down at the kitchen table and almost broke down crying. We had come so close to burning down our house that I didn't even want to think about it. Once we had calmed down, we began cleaning up the ugly mess. I remembered lecturing Mom about a small burned spot on the kitchen counter she had accidentally caused while we were away one week-end. As I looked around, I could see that this was the Lord's way of paying me back for my lack of grace and patience with my mother. I looked up with a stupid grin on my face and muttered, "You win. I'll apologize as soon as she returns home from visiting her sisters."

When it was all over, we were happy to find that there was very little damage to the kitchen, but the pot was a goner.

"I bet that chicken would have tasted good," Robbie Lee said sadly.

"Yeah, I'm still hungry. Maybe if we had a bigger pot," I started thinking. "I bet we can borrow a bigger pot from our friend Judi."

"Are you thinking of trying to deep-fry this chicken again?" Robbie Lee asked in disbelief.

"Why not? The only problem was we needed a bigger pot. Run down to Judi's and see if she has one. I know she owns every kitchen utensil ever made. She's bound to have the right size pot. Hurry, go and ask her."

Robbie Lee took off running down the street. She returned with a giant pot our friend Judi had been in the process of cooking collards in, but when she heard of our dilemma, she dumped the collards, washed the pot, and loaned it to Robbie Lee. She knows how important fried chicken is to us.

We started all over again and cooked up a beautiful fried chicken that almost melted in our mouths. Even though we nearly burned down the house, the flavor of that chicken was almost worth the trouble. I sat back with a full stomach and pictured the fire department in front of our house fighting a huge, out-of-control fire. Robbie Lee and I would be on the sidelines with pieces of chicken fixed on a wire coat hanger, holding them over the flames. When it comes to fried chicken, we're desperate people.

JUDE 1:23
"Snatch Others From The Fire And Save Them."

Have you ever gone ahead with plans to do something risky, even though you felt it was against your better judgment? With warnings ringing all around us, we still proceed because we want to satisfy our own desires rather than heed the wisdom of friends and family. The Bible teaches us everything we need to know to live and follow Christ, yet we sometimes fail to heed God's word. Our curiosity, personal pleasures, and pride guide us away from the straight path and onto what appears to be a more exciting, twisting, turning road. The problems begin when we come to turns in the road we can't navigate because we're speeding along, carefree and alone.

The book of Jude teaches us to pay attention to spiritual alarms and warnings sounded by the Holy Spirit and not to follow our ungodly desires. We may think we are in control at all times, that nothing can trip us up, but when we start thinking we don't need the counsel of others and we fail to listen to the Holy Spirit speaking to our hearts, we're heading for a fire that can burn out of control, leaving us badly burned and dazed. Listen for God's voice in His word and in godly counsel. Don't plunge into something just because you want to do it. You may get your eyebrows singed.

ADDING FIBER TO YOUR DIET

Since AC moved in with Robbie Lee and me, we've had some wonderful meals. Mom's a good cook, even if her meals do contain enough fat to kill off the entire family. It's so nice to come home from work and find dinner is on the table just waiting to be eaten. This night was no exception. Mom had fried up some pork chops, butterbeans, and French fries with homemade biscuits.

The smell in the house was wonderful. I was starving, so I threw off my coat and headed right for the kitchen. I was late getting home from work so Robbie Lee and AC were already eating in front of the television as usual, watching *Andy Griffith*. I grabbed a dish and started piling on the delicious, greasy food. When I got to the fries I couldn't help but notice there was a lot of what looked like black, burned French fries or pieces of grease. I wasn't sure which.

"Mom, what's this black stuff in the fries. Did you burn them?" I asked.

"Yeah, I think some of them got too done. But there's plenty of them that aren't burned."

"If you put ketchup on the black stuff, it actually tastes pretty good. I think it's just pieces of burned grease or something," added Robbie Lee who's known for eating any and everything that doesn't try to eat her first.

"No thanks. I think I'll pass on the black stuff," I said.

"Suit yourself, but it's not bad at all," replied AC. "While you're up, bring me another biscuit, honey, and some more of those strawberry preserves."

No matter what we have for dinner, Mom pigs out on biscuits and preserves as though they were the main meal. She eats the other food like side dishes. As I handed her the biscuit and preserves, I noticed that both she and Robbie Lee had piles of the burned black stuff on their plates.

"You guys are going to swell up and die eating that junk. Can't you see it's not good for you?" I asked.

"Oh, phooey. Everyone says everything's bad for you. I grew up on a farm, and we ate things you don't want to even think about," AC boasted.

"You're right. I don't want to know about it," I answered. "Just don't blame me when your arteries clog up, and your heart explodes."

"Please, I'm trying to eat," yelled Robbie Lee with the black gunk hanging out of her mouth.

So we settled down to our dinner of pork chops, the mysterious black blobs, and *Andy Griffith* on the television. After we finished eating, I volunteered to do the dishes since Mom cooked. As I was placing the dishes on the counter, I noticed that the mini deep fryer was out.

"Hey, Mom, you used the deep fryer for the French fries?" Mom never used any contraption like that for cooking. She had to use a frying pan for everything.

"Yeah, I didn't want to cook them the long way, so I threw them in the small deep fryer. It works OK, but they didn't taste as good as they would have cooked in a regular frying pan."

"I'm proud of you. Maybe you'll even try the microwave someday."

"Not in this lifetime. There's too much radiation pouring out of that thing. Just give me a frying pan and some oil and I'm fine."

When I finished washing the dishes, I felt the deep fryer to see if it was cool enough to put away. But I couldn't find the black plastic lid that covers it anywhere. After searching the entire kitchen, something suddenly dawned on me. *Black lid, black gunk. No, it can't be,* I thought to myself.

"Mom, could you come here for a minute?" I called.

"What's wrong?" Mom asked.

"I can't seem to find the black plastic lid that fits on the deep fryer. I was just getting ready to put it away, but the lid is missing. Do you remember where you put it while you were heating up the deep fryer?"

I could see Mom's eyes getting bigger and bigger. I was starting to get nervous. Robbie Lee, the eternal optimist, was frantically looking in all of the cabinets for the missing lid.

"Lord, have mercy!" exclaimed AC. "I never took the lid off of the deep fryer. I just plugged it in. The lid must have been on it the whole time."

"You mean it was on it for part of the time. Then it must have melted and fallen inside the deep fryer," Robbie Lee added.

"Do you realize this means that you two ate the lid to the deep fryer?" I asked.

Neither of them spoke for a moment. Then they glanced at each other and shrugged their shoulders, as if to say, "I won't tell if you won't."

"You could both get sick and die!" I screamed. "You ate cooked plastic, for heaven's sake. Don't you think we should go to the emergency room?"

"What? And tell everyone that we ate the lid to the deep fryer? I don't think so. I'll take my chances," answered AC.

Robbie Lee was scurrying off to her room.

"Where are you going?" I asked.

"To my prayer closet," Robbie Lee replied. "I figure now is a good time to catch up on my prayer time."

As she slammed the door behind her and Mom settled down on the couch to read her newspaper for the third time that day, I wondered if other families have things like this happen in their homes. I consoled myself by thinking this kind of thing probably happens to other people all the time.

We still have that same deep fryer. We cover it with a plastic zip-lock bag. Every time I take it out I think about the missing lid. I've thought about buying a new one, but I'm afraid Robbie Lee and AC might not be able to digest the lid on the newer models. It's best just keep the one we have.

ROMANS 14:3

"The Man Who Eats Everything Must Not Look Down On Him Who Does Not, And The Man Who Does Not Eat Everything Must Not Condemn The Man Who Does, For God Has Accepted Him."

In this Christian walk we're going to come across people who are a little bit different from ourselves. However, this doesn't mean that person isn't a person of strong faith. It just means they see things a tad differently than we do. Or maybe they are weaker than we are, and so they take their steps in a different order than perhaps we would take. But our role is not to judge that person and push them aside because they don't do everything to our liking. Romans 14:10 asks, "You, then, why do you judge your brother? Or why do you look down on your brother? For we all stand before God's judgment seat."

We shouldn't use ourselves as measuring sticks for others. Stop holding that person up to **your** standards and, instead, give them love and understanding. Pray for those who are weaker in their faith than you. Criticism and finger pointing will only serve to push that person further away from the Lord, not bring him or her closer. Romans 15:7 says, "Accept one another, then, just as Christ accepted you, in order to bring praise to God." If we all serve the same Lord, we should be able to walk in unity and not get sidetracked by minor differences. How much time do we waste as Christians by fighting among ourselves over trivial matters? Why not channel that energy into uniting ourselves in God's love and grace so we can show one bright light to the world?

Look past your brother or sister's tastes, likes, and dislikes. Digest the Word, and those differences will disappear. Remember, man does not live by bread alone.

SHEEPDOG SWEET POTATOES

My mom is a very good cook. Everything has to be homegrown, canned, pickled, preserved, smoked, blanched, fried, dried, and laid to the side. Since moving in with Robbie Lee and me, I believe we've both gained twenty pounds because everything Mom cooks has to be flavored with bacon grease or lard. I admit it's the best tasting food I've ever eaten, but my arteries are screaming, "HELP!"

One night when I came home from work, Mom had prepared supper and was about ready to put it on the table. I was starving to death, which is nothing unusual. Robbie Lee was already home and snooping around the kitchen, tasting everything on the stove.

"Stop eating before we sit down. You'll ruin your appetite," said Mom trying to move Robbie Lee away from the stove.

"I can't help it, I'm going to drop dead from starvation if we don't eat soon," said Robbie Lee. She's always so dramatic when it comes to eating. She's either dying from starvation or so full she's about to burst and swearing that she'll never touch another bite.

"Just sit down and I'll put everything on the table. I believe everything is ready," said Mom.

Before we sat down to eat, I noticed Mom searching all around the kitchen for something.

"What are you looking for, Mom?" I asked.

"Oh nothing, don't worry about it. Let's just eat."

I said grace and we dove right in. There was fried chicken, corn on the cob, potato salad, sweet potatoes, and biscuits that melted in my mouth.

"Mmmm, Mom, these sweet potatoes are out of this world. They have the best flavor," I said with my mouth full.

"Yeah," said Robbie Lee. That was all she could manage to get out in between stuffing her mouth full of food.

"I'm glad you like them. They had some nice-looking sweet potatoes at the store, and I just had to buy some and fix them. I knew you two would enjoy them."

While we were trying to eat, Maggie, the sheepdog, kept begging for the sweet potatoes. Every time one of us would dip into the pan for more, she would give us this pitiful look, and let out a high-pitched whine.

"What's her problem?" asked Robbie Lee. "She doesn't usually beg until after we've finished eating."

"I don't know, but she's driving me crazy. She must really like sweet potatoes or something," I replied. "Maggie, go lay down and let us eat in peace, please."

Maggie finally went to lie down under the table, but not without one final groan that sounded like she was completely exasperated.

We ate until we were "full as ticks," as my father used to say.

"You two clear the table, and I'll feed the dogs," said Mom.

We have three dogs in our house. Yes, three. We never intended to have three dogs. I used to have an Old English sheepdog named Nilsson, who died when he was thirteen years old. After he passed on, Robbie Lee decided she couldn't live without a dog, so she went down to the local ASPCA and got a mixed breed named Nicholas. He is part Dachshund and part Corgi. I love him to death, but I still missed Nilsson a lot. So I decided to go and get another Old English sheepdog, and that's how we ended up with Maggie. When Mom moved in with us, she brought her mean little white terrier named Jasper, also from the ASPCA. So we now have the three of them all living with us, in a townhouse no less.

While we were stacking the dishes, I noticed Mom was frantically searching all around the kitchen for something. She had a very confused look on her face.

"What are you looking for, Mom?" I asked.

"Maggie's supper dish, it was here a minute ago, but now I can't find it."

Maggie's dish is actually a metal baking pan with teeth marks all around it. All the dogs were lined up patiently waiting while we continued our search for the lost pan. Maggie looked pretty upset. She didn't know whether she was going to get to eat or not.

"Where's the last place you saw it, Mom?" I asked.

"It was on the floor, and I picked it up and put it on the counter so I could mop. I don't remember seeing it since."

"Do you remember putting it back down on the floor?" Robbie Lee asked.

"No, but I must have because it's not on the kitchen counter anywhere."

"OK, Mom, try to think. Do you remember moving it some place out of the way?" I asked.

"No, I just remember picking it up off the floor and putting it on the counter."

"How strange," replied Robbie Lee. "It's like it just disappeared into thin air. Maybe Maggie ate it."

As I looked all around the room, my eyes suddenly came to rest on the pan of sweet potatoes that was sitting on the table. We had eaten all of them except for a few tiny pieces. I took a closer look. It was also a square metal baking pan, but this one looked pretty beat-up. Looking even closer, I couldn't believe my eyes. Were those teeth marks on the sides?

"Oh my goodness, it's awful. We've been poisoned," I gasped.

"What on Earth are you talking about?" asked Robbie Lee.

"Just take a good look at the pan that Mom cooked the sweet potatoes in!" I cried, pointing to the table.

"Oh, no, it can't be. Say it isn't so," pleaded Robbie Lee.

"Say what isn't so?" asked Mom, oblivious to what had happened.

"You must have cooked the sweet potatoes in Maggie's supper dish!" I said.

"I did no such thing! I wouldn't cook sweet potatoes in a dog's dish," Mom said firmly.

"But you did. It was sitting on the counter and you probably just forgot it belonged to Maggie and, and, and, oh, I can't even believe it. You cooked the sweet potatoes in her dish and we ATE THEM!" I screamed.

"I know the difference between a baking pan and a dog dish, and I didn't use Maggie's dish. Besides, we have three or four of those pans around here. How can you be so sure this one belongs to Maggie?"

"Because it has teeth marks on it, Maggie's teeth marks, and the fact that her supper dish is missing is enough evidence for me," I replied.

"No wonder Maggie was begging for the sweet potatoes at the table," said Robbie Lee. "We were eating out of her dish, so she probably thought the least we could do was share with her."

"Oh, no, we're all going to die. I feel ill," I said, groaning.

"You're not going to die. A few dog germs never hurt anybody. Besides, you both bragged about how good they tasted. After all, they're all gone."

I immediately went to the store and bought Maggie a regular round dog dish so there would never be any more confusion about which was ours and which was hers. All I could taste for the rest of the night was sweet potatoes, only now the taste made me feel nauseous. To think of all the sheepdog slobber mixed in with those potatoes that we, excuse the pun, woofed down, was too much to stomach.

They were probably the best sweet potatoes I ever ate. We call them "Mom's sheepdog sweet potatoes." The secret is to use a really well-seasoned Old English sheepdog supper dish. But that's one recipe we won't be holding onto.

ROMANS 14:14

"As One Who Is In The Lord Jesus, I Am Fully Convinced That No Food Is Unclean In Itself. But If Anyone Regards Something As Unclean, Then For Him It Is Unclean."

Have you ever eaten something and then wished you hadn't? A waiter brought me a seafood platter once, and I ate everything on it and licked the plate clean. Afterwards I found out there were frog legs on the platter. Now I hate frogs. I'm also very afraid of them. The thought of eating one left me feeling more than a little sick to my stomach. So now, if the ingredients aren't listed on the menu, I ask before I order.

As Christians, we sometimes leap after things (pardon the pun). We don't stop to find out all the facts before we swallow the juicy bit of gossip we've just heard, and then we're ever so quick to share it with others. Later, after we've heard the real story, we find ourselves regretting that we even listened to the busybody who filled our ears with all of that dirt in the first place. We wish we had asked questions or maybe just skipped that little morsel altogether.

The next time you feel the urge to spread some gossip around or even listen to it, remember, it may taste like chicken, but it's still slimy frog legs. Just say, "No thank-you and pass the bread (of life)."

LIKE A SLUG IN THE MUD

Robbie Lee and I were just getting in from a long day at work.

"How about going out to eat tonight?" I asked.

"Sounds good to me," answered Robbie Lee. "But let's go somewhere that serves fried chicken."

"Fried chicken, fried chicken, is that all you ever want to eat? I think I feel like seafood tonight. Hey, there's a seafood restaurant not too far from here that we've never been to. I hear it's right on the water. How about going there tonight?" I said with a bit of adventure in my voice.

"All right then, seafood is OK. They may have a combination seafood and fried chicken plate. Some places serve that, you know."

"That girl is going to turn into fried chicken one night because her brain is already deep-fried," I mumbled to myself. "Mom, we're going out to eat some seafood tonight. Would you like to join us?" I asked while quickly changing clothes.

"Well, I guess so. Do we go by any flower nurseries on the way? I need to get some daffneydils for my garden," AC beamed.

"No, we don't pass any nurseries on the way that I know of. And besides, they're not daffneydils, they're called daffodils. Every time we go out we don't have to stop to look at flowers, do we? Just say whether or not you want to go out to eat," I answered with my eyes rolling behind AC's back.

"She won't let me go where they have fried chicken either, Mom," said Robbie Lee loud enough for me to hear.

"Let's just go, please," I said, holding open the front door.

The seafood restaurant sat on the banks of a creek in Portsmouth, VA. It was octagonal with glass windows all the way around. Robbie Lee, AC, and I were the first to arrive.

"We must be early or something," I observed, looking all around the parking lot. There was one waitress inside standing in the center of the restaurant, leaning up against the counter. Reaching the top of the stairs, we tried to open the first door we came to. It was locked. The waitress casually looked at us and then back down at a magazine.

"I don't think they're open yet," said Robbie Lee.

"Of course they're open. It's after 5 PM. Everybody's open after 5 PM," I stated with great confidence. "We'll just try another door."

So we walked around a little further until we came to another door. However, this one had a table in front of it.

"I don't think we can go in here," said Robbie Lee.

"This is crazy. There has to be a way in. Let's try another door."

So we walked around a little further to the back of the restaurant. Now the waitress inside was beginning to follow us with her eyes, watching curiously from where she stood. At the back of the restaurant we were still visible because of the glass windows all the way around.

I shook the handle of another door. It was locked as well.

"This is the most bizarre thing I have ever seen. Here stands the three of us, grown adults, wanting to go into a restaurant to eat, but we can't figure out how to get in!" I shouted at no one in particular.

"We should have gone to Kentucky Fried Chicken. We know how to get in there," said Robbie Lee.

By now AC had lost total interest and was just staring off into space like she sometimes does, probably thinking about "daffneydils."

"Let's go the rest of the way around. Maybe we just started off in the wrong direction," I suggested.

We stepped down off of the deck and continued around the restaurant. Since the water surrounded the back portion of the building, we stepped into a lot of mud. There were large pieces of wood in the mud like steps. AC and I were out in front after carefully using the wooden steps to get around to the other side of the restaurant.

"I think I see the door!" I shouted. "Robbie Lee, where are you?"

Just then, AC and I heard a loud splat. Yes, it sounded just like a splat!

"What in the world?" Retracing my careful steps toward the back of the restaurant, I saw Robbie Lee lying spread eagle on her back, like a slug in the deep mud.

"Robbie Lee, get up," I pleaded.

"I can't. I think I'm stuck," cried Robbie Lee.

"Lord, have mercy!" cried AC.

"Mom, go back or you'll wind up stuck too," I cautioned, while frantically trying to get to Robbie Lee.

The waitress was now totally engrossed in what was going on outside the back of the restaurant. She was probably starting to feel a bit nervous. Who were these people, and why were they walking around the restaurant?

"Here, grab my hand," I said, reaching out to Robbie Lee. I managed to pull her up out of the mud and guided her to dry ground. Robbie Lee was dripping mud from the top of her head to the heels of her feet.

"How in the world did you end up flat in the mud?"

"I don't know. I was trying to step carefully, but I stepped on a slippery piece of wood. The next thing I knew, I was flat on my back," explained Robbie Lee, trying to wipe away some of the mud from her hands.

"Well, I found the front door. It's right up there," I said, pointing the way. "You can clean up in the restroom inside. It's not that bad."

"You're crazy if you think I'm going in there now!"

The waitress had now moved closer for a better look, keeping one hand on the phone to dial 911 if need be.

"Robbie Lee, I'm starving to death, and now you're telling me that just because of a little mud we're not going to go in and eat!?" I screamed.

Robbie Lee stood dripping with mud, not believing that I actually expected her to just waltz into the restaurant and ask where the restroom was, wipe off a little mud, sit down, and eat.

"I'm leaving," she said, running in tears back to the car.

I ran behind her trying to convince her to stay. AC just stood and stared out into space.

"Mom, would you please come on. We're leaving now!" I shouted while waving my arms frantically in the air.

AC smiled as she walked back to the car, knowing that we would probably stop at Kentucky Fried Chicken and then run up to K-Mart and look at the daffneydils, I mean daffodils.

PSALMS 40:2

"He Lifted Me Out Of The Slimy Pit, Out Of The Mud And Mire: He Set My Feet On A Rock And Gave Me A Firm Place To Stand."

Have you ever cried out to God for help? I remember sitting on the side of my bed, feeling like the world around me was falling apart. I had several excuses for not going to church regularly, until I stopped going altogether. This decision had a great impact on my Christian walk. Robbie Lee and I had always been the best of friends, in addition to being sisters, but we had a terrible fight and we weren't on speaking terms. Without realizing it, we had drifted away from our Christian beliefs and had chosen, little by little, to adopt a world view of life rather than a Word view. We had become more concerned about what was politically correct or acceptable by society standards rather than by Biblical standards. It's amazing how much my life had changed direction as a result of, what seemed like, insignificant decisions along the way. My eyes fell on an old dusty Bible sitting on my nightstand that I hadn't read for many years. It just sat by my bed night after night while I lay there crying my eyes out and wondering why my life was in such confusion. Maybe if I had opened the book I would have found all of the answers to my questions. Instead, I paced back and forth in my room, wringing my hands in desperation.

However, on this particular night, it caught my eye. Something clicked inside of me. As I picked it up and thumbed through its pages, I saw promise after promise from God to me. It hadn't changed in all of those years sitting by my bed. God hadn't revised it or changed any of the truths I had read years ago. They were still the same. While everything around me was shifting and changing, God's Word was constant and unchanging. I had changed by walking away from God years before, but there He was, sitting by my bed. The Creator of all the universe was sitting right there all of the time, with promises, hope, and a future for me to reach out and accept.

Even though I had allowed my life to become bogged down in mud and unstable ground, He lifted me out in one quick motion and stood me on solid ground. The funny thing is, I thought I had been walking on solid ground all along. It wasn't until I got stuck in the mire, unable to get up by myself, that I realized where I was. With no hesitation, lectures, or "I told you so," He lifted me up. I had been walking around in circles, thinking I was making a lot of progress.

But instead of moving forward, I was slowly sinking. When God opened my eyes, I could easily see the way I needed to go, but before that, I couldn't see I had lost my way. I thought I had arrived, but I was really searching for the way.

Isn't it great to know that even though we walk away from God and wander around in circles for awhile that He will be standing right there to take our hand and pull us out of our muddy tracks, and place us right in front of the door to everlasting life? Are you wandering in circles thinking you're going somewhere? Take a look around. Can't you see the mud? Don't panic. He's right beside you, waiting to pull you up on your feet.

START WITH A SOLID FOUNDATION

Robbie Lee was hard at work one day in her office when she decided there was something she needed to discuss with her boss. She gathered all her materials and started to enter his office, but there were already several people in with him, and they looked pretty important. This was her boss' first day back to work from a short absence, and she didn't want to put more of a burden on him. Deciding not to bother him, she turned to leave.

"Robbie Lee, come on in. These folks were just leaving. Do you need to see me?" he asked.

"Well, yeah. I do need to discuss something with you, but I can come back later if you like."

"Nonsense, my time is your time. Come on in. What's your problem?"

Robbie Lee looked around for a place to sit, but the people who were leaving were folding up chairs and taking them out. She decided to balance herself on the end of her boss' desk just to keep out of their way.

"You see, I have this situation here that needs attention."

"Yes?"

"Yes, I'm having some difficulty with some figures in this report, and I wanted to go over the numbers with you before I went any further."

"All right then, let me have a look at them," her boss said.

Robbie Lee looked all around his office while he was studying the figures, still balanced slightly on the edge of his desk.

"Oh, here's the problem, right here," he pointed out.

"No, I thought that was the problem too, until I looked this up. You see, that can't be the problem because this says it's not," she said, handing him another piece of paper.

"Oh, yes, you're right. That can't be the problem. It has to be something else."

They both looked very serious as they pored over the numbers in the report. Robbie Lee was actually looking at the numbers upside down because of how she was sitting on the desk, but she could still decipher them.

"What about here? Couldn't this be changed to this?" her boss asked.

"No, because when you change that number, then this is off. See here?" Robbie Lee again pointed out.

"This is starting to give me a headache," her boss said.

"My head's been hurting all week. This thing's about to drive me nuts," replied Robbie Lee.

"Well, the only solution I can see is to delete these numbers, and then move these down here, like this."

"Hmmm. That might work," said Robbie Lee. She leaned a little closer to the paper to make sure she was reading it correctly. Her feet were not touching the ground, so her full weight was now resting on the corner of her boss's desk.

Suddenly, without any warning, there was a loud crash. As her boss looked up from the report, there lay Robbie Lee on top of his desk, which was now completely collapsed on the floor. He stared in disbelief over the top of his bifocals at Robbie Lee, who was sprawled spread-eagled on his desktop. There she lay amongst the papers, forms, paper clips, and stapler.

"What happened? Are you all right?" he asked, jumping to his feet.

"No, actually, I'm not all right. I think I've got a hitch in my get-along," replied Robbie Lee struggling to get to her feet.

"I can't believe my whole desk broke," her boss said in amazement.

"Neither can I," mumbled Robbie Lee.

"Hey everybody, come see this. Robbie Lee was sitting on the corner of my desk, and the whole thing collapsed!"

People came from everywhere to marvel at the sight. Robbie Lee slowly made it to her feet. She felt a bit stiff, but otherwise she was fine. She wasn't sure she wanted this story floating around the office, however.

"Say Robbie Lee, maybe you'd better think about going on a diet," a coworker said loudly.

"Yeah, it appears so," another chimed in.

"Just shut up and go back to work!" yelled Robbie Lee. It was obviously the fault of shabby workmanship that made the desk fall.

"Maybe we should finish discussing our little problem tomorrow, Robbie Lee," said her boss, surveying the huge mess in his office. "This could take some time to put back together."

"Yeah sure, whatever you say, boss," replied Robbie Lee as she limped back to her desk.

"Robbie Lee, I think you should fill out this here accident report in case you've hurt yourself and don't know it. It could bother you later on, and this way you'll be covered in case you need workers' compensation," said the boss's secretary. She walked away smiling behind Robbie Lee's back.

"Hmmph, accident report, she just wants me to put this down in black-and-white so she can file it under *gossip!*" screamed Robbie Lee. "Maybe she's right. I'd better fill it out. I may have broken something I'll need later."

As she began completing the form, she had to chuckle to herself while answering the first question.

"'One. What is the nature of the accident?' I sat on my boss's desk, and it collapsed. Oh, boy. That sounds lovely. I think I'll just take the rest of the day off."

Robbie Lee picked up her bag and wandered to the door to leave. She heard several coworkers laughing quietly in the background as she passed.

"Deadbeats. They've got nothing better to do than laugh at the misfortune of others," Robbie Lee mumbled.

As she exited the building, she passed a friend from another office.

"Tough day?" she asked.

"Yeah, you could say that," responded Robbie Lee, wondering how she could tell.

As she walked to her car, her friend watched from the door.

"Hey, how'd you get paper clips stuck in your hair?" she yelled.

"Never mind," Robbie Lee yelled back as she walked to the parking lot. "That's it. Now I've got to find another job, all because of some flimsy desk. Boy, they sure don't build them like they used to."

But all the way home she kept wondering just how well the Slim·Fast drinks really work.

PROVERBS 24:16
"For Though A Righteous Man Falls Seven Times, He Rises Again, But The Wicked Are Brought Down By Calamity."

It's always hard to get back up after a fall, especially if you keep falling in the same place. We get angry with ourselves, and sometimes we become discouraged and give up. But we're not perfect and God knows that. After all, He created us. He knows our faults and our weaknesses and He knows we're going to stumble and sometimes even collapse for a while. Don't beat yourself up when this happens; it will only make you stay down longer. We have God on our side, and He's not going to give up on us. Like a baby learning to walk, we have to get back up again and again, but He's right there encouraging us with His word and His grace.

Sometimes our enemies cause us to fall with a careless word or action, and we're so shocked because we don't think it will ever happen to us. When it does, we want revenge. We want to see our enemies fall too, but Proverbs 24:17 says, "Do not gloat when your enemy falls; when he stumbles, do not let your heart rejoice, or the Lord will see and disapprove and turn His wrath away from him." What a raw deal. You mean if we fall, we just have to get back up, but if our enemy falls, we can't even party for a little while? The two key words here are righteous and enemy. God says that even though we stumble and fall, He allows us the grace to get back up and get right back in line. Suppose He gloated and said, "Serves you right. You had it coming." We would never make it. It's through His grace that we stand again, and so He expects the same grace from us concerning our enemies. We are to love our enemies, not dance on their bodies while they're down. Yes, God does have a higher standard for His people. That's what makes us different from the world. Anybody can hate their enemies and love their friends. But God asks us to go beyond what the world practices, and let His love shine through our daily actions.

When you fall, get back up. God's grace allows for it. When your enemy falls, don't rejoice, give him a hand. Who knows where it might lead?

KNOCK, KNOCK, WHO'S THERE?

Most normal people are able to stay in hotels without any problems whatsoever, but that doesn't seem to be the case with my family. For some reason, wherever we go, we never lack at least one embarrassing event. Don't go thinking we're crazy or anything. We just seem to be tested more than others. I'm sure we'll be better for it in the long run.

Sometime back, there was a week-long revival meeting with a speaker we really wanted to hear. The meeting was to be held almost twenty-five miles from where we lived. Rather than drive back and forth every night for the week, we decided to check into a hotel closer by. Besides being more convenient, it would make us feel like we were away from home and add more excitement to the whole event.

Now when it comes to packing, Robbie Lee is at her peak of expertise. This woman writes out lists of things to bring before she even begins to pack. She coordinates colors and only packs the needed number of outfits for each day. You know the type, "I'll wear this on Monday and this pretty little outfit on Tuesday, etc." When you walk in her room, she has each outfit laid out with a pair of socks, underwear, and any needed accessories. As she places each item in her suitcase, she checks it off her handy list, humming as she goes along. I can't watch for very long before I become very nauseous.

I, on the other hand, can never decide what to bring. I stand in my closet for hours just trying to decide if I even like an item well enough to take it on a trip with me, trying to envision myself wearing each piece of clothing. My biggest hang-up is I'm afraid I'll get away from home and hate everything I brought to wear. So I bring what I like to call "just-in-case" clothes. I usually need more than one suitcase when I'm finished, but it's worth the trouble.

AC is the worst of the lot. It doesn't take her any time to pack because she just goes into her closet and pulls out everything she owns. She does this whether she's going away for a week or only one night. Not only does she bring everything, but she leaves it all on hangers instead of putting them in her suitcase. Her suitcase is reserved for underwear and a wide variety of plastic bags that hold makeup, medicine, facial creams, and Lord knows what else. AC actually doesn't understand the concept of a suitcase. She insists on putting everything in a plastic bag before it's packed. This is so she can drive us crazy late at night in the room while she rummages through each one, making lots of noise.

When we finally arrived at the hotel, the check-in process went just fine. We were told that our room was ready, and the desk clerk carefully gave us instructions on how to get to it. Of course, none of us paid any attention. We all stared at the woman, shaking our heads while saying, "Uh-huh. Uh-huh." But when everything was said and done, not one of us could remember what she said. We each remembered bits and pieces of her instructions, so we figured we'd manage.

Our room was located in another building. We piled back into the car and while we all talked at once, we drove like madwomen all over the parking lot until we finally arrived at the right spot. Of course, getting the clothes out of the car is always a disaster. AC is a small, petite woman, and she's not able to handle very much weight. So she usually ends up carrying one small bag, and Robbie Lee and I get stuck with the entire contents of her closet. I don't like to make two trips, so I insisted that we carry everything up at once.

Loaded down with hanging clothes, suitcases, and the many spare shoes, we started out to find our room. Robbie Lee and AC remembered the room number, and they had the key.

"The room number is 328," Robbie Lee yelled back at me.

"Wait, why are you going that way?" I asked.

"Because this is the way the woman said to go," replied Robbie Lee. "Weren't you listening?"

"Yes, but I think I'm going to take the stairs instead of walking the length of the hallway to find an elevator. It'll be shorter."

"Suit yourself, but I think you're making a big mistake."

"You take AC with you. I'll meet ya'll there."

So we separated. I headed up the stairs, barely able to walk with the load I'm carrying. I watched as Robbie Lee struggled with her baggage, walking behind AC who looked like she was the queen of the hotel carrying her one small bag. Before long, I was exhausted, and I didn't think I could take another step. The stairs nearly killed me. I called AC names under my breath with every painful step I took. Finally I saw the room number, 328. The door was already half open.

"Oh, good, they're already in there." I thought.

With one swift kick, I flung open the door and ran to the first bed I saw, throwing down everything I had in my arms.

"Whew! I made it. I didn't think I was going to be able to take another step."

As I looked up, there sat an elderly man with white hair in his bathrobe. He was sitting in the corner of the room with the television remote control in his hand. His eyes were as wide as saucers, and he looked like he had just seen a ghost. He pointed the remote at me as if to say, "Take one more step, baby, and I'll mute you."

"I'm so sorry," I said, picking up my suitcases and hanging clothes. "I must have the wrong room. I'm leaving right away."

As I struggled with the bags and the door, I knew the old man must have been thinking I would never leave his room. He never moved from his chair and kept the remote control on me the whole time. When I finally fell outside into the hallway, I just burst out laughing until I start to cry. I couldn't help but see the expression on that man's face over and over again in my mind. I'm sure he was calling the front desk complaining about this crazy woman who barged into his room and was now having some kind of fit outside his door.

I finally managed to drag myself down the hall until I saw Robbie Lee and AC standing outside our door.

"Where have you been? We were getting worried," said Robbie Lee.

"You gave me the wrong room number. I've just been down the hall terrorizing an elderly gentleman."

"Yeah, I know. I knocked on the wrong door too. A man answered the door wearing a towel. He must've just gotten out of the shower. I apologized and left. We finally discovered the right room number scribbled on a piece of paper the woman had given us."

"Hurry up and put the bags down so we can go eat," added AC in her helpful manner.

Later that evening during the revival meeting, I saw the elderly man I scared half to death going up for prayer. I reckon he figured he'd better not take any chances while there was a wild woman roaming the halls of the hotel.

GALATIANS 6:5
"For Each One Should Carry His Own Load."

Ever tried taking on more than you can handle? It's so easy to do. At the time it all seems manageable to you, but down the road you find yourself burdened down with not only your load, but everyone else's as well. Christians always seem to feel that if they do more work, God will love them more. The truth is He just wants a relationship with us, and no amount of work we do will make that relationship better. But still we take it all on. We say, "Maybe if I do this in addition to this thing over here, God will look down and say, 'My, I sure do love that little son or daughter of mine. They just work, work, work.'" In reality, He's looking down and saying, "Hey, I wonder when my son or daughter is going to stop running around in circles and spend some time with me."

It's important to learn how to say no. We tend to feel guilty if we have to turn someone down even when we know we're filled to capacity and can't handle any more. Instead, we find ourselves letting "yes" leak from our mouths far too many times. Now don't get me wrong, I'm not saying you should never volunteer for anything. I'm just saying learn to weigh the load you are already carrying against the additional load someone's asking you to take on. If you don't, you may find yourself with no time left for your family, yourself, or your Lord. You'll start to feel empty, burned-out, and unsatisfied.

Slow down. Carry a manageable load. Learn to say "no." Spend time working on your relationship with Christ. Everything else will fall into place.

STEWED AT A PARTY

Some years back, Robbie Lee and I lived across the street from an elderly couple with whom we had become great friends. Their names were Ann and Larry, and they were the sweetest couple you could hope to meet. Well, Ann and Larry were celebrating their fiftieth wedding anniversary, and they were nice enough to invite us.

I'm not a party kind of person, but this was such a special occasion that I made an exception and decided to attend. Robbie Lee made up her mind immediately to attend because the party was to include a full buffet, and she never passes up the chance to socialize over hot food or, for that matter, cold food.

"You know, I haven't a thing to wear to this gala affair," I said, looking through my closet. "None of these clothes are befitting such a party as this."

"I'm going to wear something that stretches," said Robbie Lee, closing her eyes and dreaming of the spread that would be on the table.

"That figures. Well, I'm going shopping to buy me just the right outfit for the party."

With that, I headed out the door for the mall while Robbie Lee popped another Famous Amos chocolate chip cookie in her mouth. When I returned, I was so pleased to show off my new purchases.

"I found this great cream sweater and this blue skirt. I'm going to wear this along with my pink silk blouse under the sweater. I also bought this great necklace to top it all off. Don't you just love it?" I held it up in front of the mirror, striking different poses, admiring the sweater and the long necklace together.

"Yeah, boy it's beautiful, but I still think it's best to be more practical and go with something that can adapt to a full buffet," replied Robbie Lee.

On the day of the party, I could hardly wait to wear my new outfit. I showered, did my hair and makeup, and sprayed on my favorite perfume. I slipped the creamy sweater over my pretty pink silk blouse and pulled on my blue skirt. Finally, I draped the long necklace around my neck. I was a vision.

"We best get going. We don't want to be late!" I yelled.

"I'm ready," called Robbie Lee from her room. She was wearing her black pants with the elastic waist and a baggy blouse.

"This is going to be a good party," she said as she stood in front of the mirror pulling the elastic on her pants to see how far it would stretch.

When we arrived at the church hall where the celebration was taking place, there were lots of people already there.

"I hope they haven't started eating yet," Robbie Lee said, quickening her pace into the building. I chose to stroll into the church hall smiling and waving at some of the people, giving them ample time to see my new clothes, even though I didn't actually know who they were.

Ann and Larry looked so sweet, holding hands and greeting everyone as they came inside. They had been married fifty years, and they still looked as though they adored one another. When I got inside, Robbie Lee and I chatted politely with a few folks until the announcement was made that the buffet was now open.

"Now control yourself, Robbie Lee. Don't make a pig of yourself. Just get a little of each thing on your plate," I warned her.

But it was too late. Robbie Lee was already in the buffet line filling up her plate. I just shook my head in disgust, picked up a plate, and waited my turn in line. I politely dipped up a little of each dish, smiling and chatting as I went.

After filling my plate, I decided to go and speak to some of my friends and neighbors seated around the room and show off my new outfit to those who might have missed my grand entrance. I immediately noticed that everyone seemed to be admiring the new clothes. They were talking about my new creamy sweater and especially noticed the necklace.

I have such great taste, I thought.

After going around and greeting everyone, I joined Robbie Lee, who was standing in the center of the room, eating her little heart out. As I approached her, Robbie Lee burst into laughter, with her mouth wide open, revealing sweet potatoes and fried chicken. It was a disgusting sight, to say the least.

"May I ask what is so funny? And would you mind not laughing with your mouth full of food. It's starting to make me ill, for heaven's sake."

But Robbie Lee didn't seem able to control herself. She bent over, screaming with laughter, while trying to balance her food on her plate.

"What is it? Tell me so I can laugh too. Did you hear a good joke?" By now I could see everyone was beginning to stare at us. But Robbie Lee couldn't answer. She could only point to my creamy sweater and howl.

As I looked down to see what was causing all of the hysterics, I couldn't believe my eyes. My new long necklace had strings of stewed tomatoes hanging from it, and the new creamy sweater was covered in tomato sauce from the necklace swinging back and forth around my neck. Apparently, while reaching across the buffet for a piece of fried chicken, I had dipped my lovely necklace into the stewed tomatoes, which were now hanging in strings around my neck.

My face began to burn.

I went all the way around the room and spoke to folks, I thought. Robbie Lee laughed louder. *There were tomatoes hanging from my necklace all the way around the room, and nobody said a word.*

Robbie Lee was almost on the floor now. I could feel everyone's eyes on us as we stood in the center of the room, precariously trying to look normal, with the stewed tomatoes displayed proudly on the front of my brand-new creamy sweater.

Suddenly, as if enough had not already gone wrong, a button popped off from the sleeve of my pretty, pink silk blouse, leaving it dangling wide open. Robbie Lee gasped for air as she watched my perfectly coordinated outfit seemingly fall apart before her eyes.

For a moment we stared at one another, wondering what would happen next, but then we began to howl like hyenas in the center of the room. Tears rolled down our faces as food flew from our mouths.

An elderly lady walked over to us and whispered, "You two seem to be the only ones really enjoying this party. What's your secret?"

We paused and just looked at each other, then continued to howl.

This went on for a spell until we both decided it would be best if we just left and returned home. We waved good-bye to Ann and Larry and ran off to the car. Driving home, we laughed until we cried. Robbie Lee paused long enough to ask, "Are you going to eat those stewed tomatoes around your neck?" I'm surprised she didn't rip them off of my neck and start to suck on them.

It was awhile before I could bring myself to attend any more parties. As a matter of fact, it was awhile before I was invited to any more parties. Ann and Larry never mentioned what happened, but I've heard that every time Ann sees stewed tomatoes, it reminds her of a story she repeats to her friends and even strangers to this day. At least I learned a valuable lesson about what not to wear to a buffet party.

LUKE 8:17

"For There Is Nothing Hidden That Will Not Be Disclosed, And Nothing Concealed That Will Not Be Known Or Brought Out In The Open."

Sometimes no matter how much we plan and no matter how hard we try, things fall apart and the worst side of us is exposed. We tend to let God manage only part of our lives, and we let Him know that we are perfectly capable of handling the other parts ourselves. But sooner or later, our sheltered area begins to fall apart and only then do we offer it up to Christ for his guidance and wisdom. We want God to help us find a new job, but we want to handle who we should marry. We want God to heal our illness, but we want to take care of our addiction to gossip, lying, overspending, etc.

You may think you have things well in hand. You've calculated. You've scrutinized. You've talked to your friends. You've listened to your heart. But you haven't sought out God's will for this area of your life. Maybe you're afraid of the answer He'll give, or maybe you think you shouldn't burden God with every area of your life. Besides, there are some things you already have figured out and you know what you want. Why should you bother God with them? Because He loves you and wants your whole life and your whole heart, that's why. He wants us to run everything by Him. What better counselor could you ask for than your Creator? He knows the number of hairs on your head. Why shouldn't He care about who you marry? Who you date? Your finances? Believe me, He does.

Make it a habit to run all of your decisions by Him. Learn to listen for His voice. Learn to wait on Him. Be patient. Don't wait until the things you've left hidden are exposed. Don't make your own decisions and then ask God to bless them. Check with Him first. It's easier than having your buttons pop open in public.

THE SECRET RECIPE

Arriving home from work one evening, I noticed Robbie Lee's car was already there. This was unusual because she is almost always late getting home from work. When I walked in, Robbie Lee yelled, "Surprise! I've cooked supper tonight."

Now most people would be delighted to hear such news. It means you don't have to get in the kitchen after a hard day at work and rattle those pots and pans and then wash them afterwards, but in my house it's different. Whenever Robbie Lee announces that she's cooked anything, everyone always cringes a little. You see, Robbie Lee isn't known for her cooking ability, even though when we were growing up she was the one who followed Mom all around the kitchen like mother's little helper. I've decided she must have just been going from cabinet to cabinet eating, because she sure didn't pick up any cooking skills while she was in there.

But Robbie Lee looked so excited and pleased with herself that I tried to keep quiet and acted as though I was overcome with joy.

"Oh, Robbie Lee, you didn't have to do that," I said sincerely.

"Well, you're always doing the cooking. So I decided to give you a break tonight," explained Robbie Lee, grinning from ear to ear.

"What are we having, then?" I asked, bracing myself for her answer.

"Baked chicken," she proudly replied.

Baked chicken doesn't sound bad at all, I thought to myself. *I reckon she could manage to bake a chicken without doing it too much harm. After all, it's a fairly simple meal to make. Maybe it won't be like the time she put cinnamon in the hamburger casserole, or like the time when she put six cups of rice in one cup of water to cook.*

I found myself feeling guilty that I had not taken this nice gesture to heart from the beginning instead of rolling my eyes to the back of my head. I was willing to give this meal a chance. After all, it's the thought that counts, right?

In my family, we always say grace before we eat any meals, or even snacks, because with Robbie Lee and AC around, I'll take all the protection I can get. Tonight I said an extra-long grace, figuring it couldn't hurt for this meal. Robbie Lee kept looking at me through half-opened eyes as I prayed. I know this because

I kept peeking to make sure she wasn't adding any extra touches to the food while I had my eyes closed.

As I finally got up the nerve to say amen, I opened my eyes and looked at the chicken on the table. It looked beautiful, all brown and juicy, just like a good baked chicken should look. Robbie Lee cut me off a big piece and served it with pride just beaming out of her every pore. Beside the chicken, she slapped down some mashed potatoes (a little lumpy, but tasty), some gravy (very lumpy, but tasty), and a biscuit (not lumpy, but hard). I took a deep breath and bit into the chicken with my eyes closed. Much to my surprise, it was good. It was very good. As a matter of fact, it was just about the crispiest baked chicken I had ever eaten.

"This is really good, Robbie Lee. You've outdone yourself," I said.

"Thank you, Polly D. I was a little nervous, but I guess it turned out all right."

"Oh, it's just delicious!" I exclaimed in amazement. "I believe I'll have another piece."

I couldn't believe I was saying that. I had never asked for another piece of anything Robbie Lee had baked, fried, broiled, boiled, or warmed up. But here I was, asking for seconds. Maybe somewhere along the line, all the things she watched Mom do in the kitchen had finally popped into her brain and started to work.

I ate until I was stuffed and couldn't eat another bite.

"I'll do the dishes since you cooked," I graciously offered.

"All right," Robbie Lee replied, looking exhausted from her cooking achievements.

When I got to the glass baking dish the chicken had been cooked in, I noticed there was a clear blob of something attached to the sides of it. I took out a scouring pad and started scrubbing it, but it wouldn't budge. I couldn't figure for the life of me what in the world it could be. It was clear and sticky and it wasn't coming off no matter what I used.

"Robbie Lee, could you come here for a moment?" I called.

"What's up?" she asked.

"Do you know what this clear-looking blob is on the side of this baking dish? Nothing I use will take it off. I've tried everything."

"Oh, that?" she asked pointing to the huge blob of gook on the dish.

"Yes, that. What is it?"

"It might be some of the clear plastic wrap I used to cover the chicken while it was baking."

"Clear plastic wrap? You wrapped the chicken in clear plastic wrap and then baked it in a gas oven for an hour?" I asked with my mouth hanging open wider than I thought possible.

"Yeah, and you should have seen it when the heat hit it. It shrunk all over the chicken until it looked like it just disappeared."

For a moment I couldn't say anything at all. I just stared at Robbie Lee as she stood there in front of me with this stupid, goofy grin that said, "What's the problem?" I couldn't believe I had just eaten a chicken with clear plastic wrap baked right into it. No wonder it was extra crispy!

"What in the world made you think to put plastic wrap over a chicken that you're about to put into a hot gas oven?" I asked loudly.

"Well, I've seen you use plastic wrap over food before," Robbie Lee replied with her hands placed on her hips.

"I've never baked anything covered in plastic wrap, you raving lunatic! I use the plastic wrap to cover leftovers when they're going in the refrigerator, but not to bake with. I always use aluminum foil for that."

"Ooooh," Robbie Lee said with a look on her face that said she finally understood the difference between the two. "I'll have to write that down."

"We'll probably both swell up and die before morning. Why didn't you tell me this before we ate?" I shrilled.

"Well, you couldn't tell it by looking at the chicken, so I figured it would be all right. Besides, you said a long prayer over it. We'll probably be fine."

Robbie Lee shuffled off nonchalantly back into the living room, leaving me standing alone in the kitchen with the glass baking dish and the clear plastic blob.

For a while, I couldn't bring myself to move, but eventually I just tossed the baking dish into the trash and went into the living room with Robbie Lee. There she sat, happy as a lark, in complete bliss, watching *Andy Griffith* and laughing at Floyd the barber.

All night long, every time I felt the least little twinge, I would put my fingers on the buttons of the telephone so that I would have a head start dialing 911 before I died. I didn't know whether anyone had ever died from plastic wrap poisoning or not, but I didn't want to take any chances. I whispered another prayer before I went to bed, asking the Lord to please spare us from any harm the evening's meal might bring. I didn't want the whole world to find out we died from eating Saran Wrapped Chicken. In the quiet of the night I thought I heard the Lord say to me, "This too shall pass."

PSALM 90:8
"You Have Set Our Iniquities Before You, Our Secret Sins In The Light Of Your Presence."

Have you ever done something in secret that you thought no one else would ever find out about, only to have that secret exposed to your great embarrassment? For some reason, we all tend to think that we can get away with some small sins if we just play our cards right. We think, *Oh, this is not such a bad thing. Who will know? Maybe I'll try it just this once.* But even if no one else finds out, God sees everything we do. He also sees our heart. When we take even small wrongs into our hearts, we've opened the door for more of the Enemy's plans against us.

The Holy Spirit provides us with a warning signal telling us we're heading in the wrong direction, but sometimes we ignore that warning, thinking that we're in control and we're on top of it. But that's where we go wrong. We shouldn't be in control; God should be, but we still try our best to hide some areas of our lives and run our own show behind the scenes.

Spending time with God will bring to light these small dark areas we've allowed to develop in our hearts. The more time you spend with Him, the more light will shine until you no longer feel comfortable with having these dark areas hidden in your life. Remember, even though you feel you've been successful at hiding things from others, God sees everything. There's no hiding your heart from Him. So you might as well own up and start cleaning house. Go ahead and sweep out the corners, not just the areas that everyone sees. There are no secrets with God.

HOW THE MIGHTY HAVE FALLEN

It was a Friday night, and Robbie Lee, AC, and I had plans to attend a play at Kempsville Presbyterian Church in Virginia Beach. This was before AC had moved in with us.

"Let's leave early to make sure we get good seats," I said, adding the finishing touches to my makeup.

"Well, I've been ready for an hour and now I'm waiting on you," replied Robbie Lee. She always gets dressed early, but when we're ready to go out the door, she finds a hundred things to do.

"All right, I'm ready." I said, grabbing my coat and car keys. Of course, there I stood by the front door, all alone because you-know-who wasn't ready yet. "Robbie Lee, let's go. We still have to pick up Mom, you know."

"Don't rush me. I've been ready for all this time, and now that you're ready to go, you want to push me out the door," Robbie Lee was busy doing something in her room. I could hear her walking back and forth in there.

"What on Earth are you doing? We're going to be late," I shouted at the top of my lungs. Suddenly, I heard Robbie Lee's bedroom door slam and footsteps on the stairs. She was wearing an entirely different outfit than she had on previously. "You changed clothes? I'm standing down here waiting and you change clothes?"

"I just didn't feel comfortable in that other outfit. This one is much better. Besides, we have plenty of time." Robbie Lee grabbed her coat and headed for the car. I followed closely behind, mumbling under my breath. Robbie Lee didn't pay any attention because I was always mumbling something under my breath.

When we arrived at AC's house, it was raining cats and dogs. Neither of us wanted to get out of the car, so I blew the horn to let Mom know that we were there. I had called her ahead of time, as we always did, to let her know we were on the way, and she was given strict instructions to be ready and watching.

"Do you think she heard the horn?" I asked, growing impatient.

"Try it again. You know she doesn't hear well," said Robbie Lee.

So I leaned down on the horn for a long time, but there was no movement in the house. It began to rain harder now. I tried the horn one more time, but there was still no sign of AC.

"She knows we're coming. Why isn't she watching for us out of the window?" I began gritting my teeth as I sometimes do when I'm about to explode.

"One of us is going to have to go after her," Robbie Lee pointed out, but not initiating any movement to get out of the car.

"Well, which one do you think should go?"

"I can't go," replied Robbie Lee. "If I get out in this rain, my hair will frizz up like one big fuzz ball." She checked her hairdo in the rearview mirror to make sure it was still in place.

"And I suppose my hair won't be affected at all?" I asked sarcastically.

"Not like mine. You know your hair is thicker than mine. Yours holds up much better in humidity than my thin hair does." Robbie Lee continued looking in the mirror and didn't even notice I was giving her a killer look.

"All right, all right, I'll go, but she'd better be ready." I threw a newspaper over my head, as if that would do any good, darted out of the car and up the stairs to the house. I banged on the door as hard as I could, but there was no answer. Looking through the kitchen window, I could see no sign of AC. I was really steaming now, and was beginning to fantasize about what I was going to do once I got hold of her.

Now I'm not known for being very graceful, especially when wearing heels. When I turned to go back down the steps, thinking maybe I would go around back and bang on the den window for awhile, my foot slipped and I danced all the way down the steps and onto the driveway. My shoes fell off and landed in the rain, where they began to fill up with water. On top of everything else, I had turned my foot and wasn't able to get up right away. My dress was every which way but down, as the wind and rain soaked me right through to the bone.

"I wonder if Robbie Lee saw me fall. To be sure she'll come and help me up," I mumbled while lying lifeless in the driveway.

Robbie Lee saw me fall, but she still wasn't going to get out of the car unless it was absolutely necessary. She kept wiping the window of the car to see if she could detect any movement in my lifeless body, but she could see I wasn't moving. I stared up at the rain falling in my face. Then I began thinking how bizarre it would be if I were to die right here on the driveway of my mother's home, with dear Mom dry and warm inside the house and my dear, sweet sister still sitting in the car.

More time passed and Robbie Lee could see that I was not getting up any time soon.

"I can't believe I have to get out in this mess. When I get AC in front of me, I'm going to strangle her until her hair falls out," she said. With that, Robbie Lee jumped out of the car and into the pouring rain.

When she reached me, she politely jumped over me, leaving me lying in the rain.

"Could you at least hand me my shoes?" I pleaded.

She obliged me by running back for my shoes, flinging them at me.

"Are you OK?" she asked me without stopping to find out.

She was on a mission. Robbie Lee ran to the back of the house and looked through the den window. There was AC, warm and dry, swaying back and forth to her favorite country music videos. Robbie Lee growled. Yes, she actually growled. With all of her might, she banged on the den window. AC is very hard of hearing, so she had the television up pretty loud, plus she was singing at the top of her lungs. Robbie Lee looked around for a stick, but fortunately there was a break in the music. She banged on the window again and AC turned and screamed at the sight of Robbie Lee, dripping wet, eyes glaring, and teeth shining through her den window.

AC opened the window.

"Why didn't you knock on the front door?" she asked.

Robbie Lee spewed words that were not understandable to AC or, for that matter, to anyone. She did, however, manage to motion for AC to go to the door and let her in. When AC opened the door, she could see me lying in the driveway, in the same position that I had landed.

"Aren't you going to the play?" AC asked very innocently.

I just moaned. Robbie Lee made it through the front door by this time, and I've never heard such carrying on in my life. She was waving her arms, spitting, and acting like a wild woman. Somehow I had managed to drag myself up off the ground and hobble into the kitchen. I looked like a drowned rat with runny makeup.

AC wasn't saying much, because she was too busy staring at Robbie Lee's frizzy hair.

"Is it raining outside?" she asked. Just as Robbie Lee started to lunge at AC, I grabbed her coat and dragged her a safe distance away.

"Now everyone just calm down," I yelled. "Mom, get your coat on, and let's get in the car and go to this stupid play."

While AC was getting her coat, I felt a sharp pain in my toes, so I removed my shoe.

"Robbie Lee, do you think my toes are broken?" I asked, holding my foot up for her to see.

With great sensitivity, Robbie Lee took one look at my foot and smiled, "With those toes, who could tell?" Then she burst into hysterical laughter.

I just sat and stared, figuring Robbie Lee had just flipped out. So I decided not to take the remark personally.

"I'm ready now," said AC, standing with her coat on and a perfectly dry hairdo.

As I was limping to the car, I could hear Robbie Lee cracking up in fits of laughter, repeating over and over again, "With your toes, who could tell?" On the way to the play, I'm sure AC wondered whether or not her two daughters needed professional help. We certainly needed new hairdos.

EZEKIEL 7:5
"This Is What The Sovereign Lord Says: Disaster! An Unheard-Of Disaster Is Coming."

Some days start off perfectly. You wake up. The birds are singing. The sun is shining. Your hair falls just right. You have a great day at the office. There's no traffic on the drive home. Everything is just perfect. Little do you know that right around the corner, there is a disaster waiting for you to run right smack dab into it. You're unprepared. Who could have seen it coming? How could God allow this to happen? Why didn't He say what was coming?

Life is filled with ups and downs. Sometimes we wait until we're in the middle of a crisis before we call on God. Wouldn't it be easier if we communicated with Him all of the time and not just in our desperate time of need? He loves us. But we tend to ignore Him when everything is going our way. Does God do things to get our attention? Sometimes, especially when it's the only way He can get us to stop, look up, and spend time with Him.

Are things going your way today? Well, how about taking a little time to tell Him how much you love Him and to thank Him for the good day? You'll be surprised at how much stronger you'll feel during the times of crisis because you spent time with Him before trouble turned the corner.

THE MYSTERY OF THE
CLOGGED PIPE

One morning while going through my daily routine, I flushed the toilet and heard a strange gushing sound. Then, like a mini volcano, water exploded up and onto the floor all around my bare feet.

"Ahhhh! It's a flood!" I screamed, as I tore the bathroom closet apart looking for the plunger.

"What's all of the commotion about in here?" asked Robbie Lee. "Oh my goodness, there's water everywhere. What happened?"

"I don't know. All I did was flush the toilet and the next thing I know I'm drowning."

"Did you try the plunger?"

"I'm just about to do that now. Out of my way."

Now I'm of the belief that most any stopped-up drain can be unclogged with a trusty plunger. Getting a firm grip on the handle, I positioned the plunger over the toilet and began the necessary up-and-down motion with great vigor.

"There, that should do it!" I exclaimed after at least ten minutes of pushing and pulling. I boldly pressed the toilet handle and stood back with my arms folded with pride. But instead of magically disappearing, the water came up around the rim and began to drip out onto the floor.

"No, no, don't come out. Please, stay in there," I begged.

"Are we talking to the toilet now?" asked Robbie Lee.

"I don't understand it. I plunged it properly. It should be working now."

"Maybe you didn't do it right."

"Of course I did it right. There's only one way to do it."

"Well then, the water should be going down instead of up and over," Robbie Lee said, smiling devilishly.

"This calls for desperate action. I'm going to the Food Lion. I'll be right back."

"Food Lion? What for?"

"I'm going to buy gallons of Liquid Plumber. That'll fix it for sure."

When I returned home, I poured bottle after bottle of the liquid down the toilet, but there was no change. The water just stood in the bowl, sloshing back and forth, dripping onto the floor.

"Still no luck?" asked Robbie Lee.

"There must be a big problem down there. Nothing I've done seems to work."

"Maybe if we just leave it alone for a while it'll unstop itself."

"Are you crazy? A toilet never unstops itself. We're going to have to call a for real plumber."

"But won't that cost a lot of money? After all, it's Saturday."

"We don't have a choice. We have to do something. It's the only bathroom we have. Give me the yellow pages and stand aside."

I felt overwhelmed as I flipped through the phone book and saw how many different ads there were for plumbers. There were short ads, long ads, big ads, *huge ads*, all promising to be fast, on time, available twenty-four hours, licensed, reliable, trustworthy, etc., etc. But none of them promised to be affordable. I closed my eyes and just picked one at random, hoping for a stroke of luck.

While Robbie Lee and I waited for the plumber to arrive, we sat down and had some breakfast. I kept mumbling, in between bites of eggs and toast, that I couldn't imagine what could be causing the toilet to be in such a mess. Robbie Lee just kept her mouth filled with food, managing a grunt of acknowledgment every once in a while. I always find it very frustrating when I can't figure out a problem on my own, especially when I've tried all of the proven techniques.

Finally the plumber arrived and I followed him around, watching his every move. I like to observe workers doing their job so I can pick up little tips here and there for later use. But I could tell I was beginning to get on his nerves with all my questions and breathing down his neck, so I decided to leave him be for a while. A few minutes later, he came into the house.

"Ladies, could ya'll step outside here for a minute. I'd like to show you something," he said.

We followed the lanky man out into the yard and around the side of the house. We all knelt down around a pipe sticking out of the siding, like Indians around a campfire.

"Now this here is your clean-out valve. I've been running this here long snakelike deal through this pipe to clean it out, and look here what I found."

As he reached his hand inside the pipe, my heart began to pound a little. What would he pull out? Money? Jewelry? A dead animal? What?

"I found this washrag in your pipe. That's what's been causing all your problems."

"A washrag? How did a washrag get into the pipe?" I asked with great curiosity.

"Could it have gotten there from the washing machine?" asked Robbie Lee with a strange look on her face.

"No, I don't see how that's possible," replied the plumber with authority.

"A washrag?" I kept repeating. "How in the world?"

"I'll go out to my truck and write up your bill," said the plumber. "I'll be right back."

"Take your time," I replied.

Robbie Lee and I walked back into the house. I stood in the middle of the living room scratching my head, still trying to figure out the puzzle of the mysterious washrag.

"I just can't imagine in my wildest dreams how a wash rag—"

"All right, all right, I confess," Robbie Lee blurted out. "I did it. It was me. I'm the culprit."

"You? What are you talking about?" I asked.

"I was washing around the toilet last night when I suddenly noticed that the washrag I was using was missing. I looked all over for it, but I couldn't find it. I just went to bed and forgot about it, until Mr. Plumber dragged it out of that pipe."

"You mean you watched me plunge my brains out, spend money on liquid stuff to pour down the drain and now a plumber, and you knew all along what the problem was?" I couldn't believe I was deceived by my very own flesh and blood.

"No, I mean, I didn't think about it being the washrag until the plumber showed it to us. Honestly, I didn't," Robbie Lee said firmly.

We split the bill in half between us, and I gave Robbie Lee the benefit of the doubt. But to this day, I'm still not sure she wasn't just keeping quiet about the washrag, praying it would dissolve somehow and disappear. She still maintains her innocence, but there always seems to be a mischievous smile on her face whenever the subject is brought up. Now every time the toilet gets stopped up, Robbie Lee is the first one we blame.

COLOSSIANS 1:26
"The Mystery That Has Been Kept Hidden For Ages And Generations, But Is Now Disclosed To The Saints."

I love a good mystery. I guess I have a bit of a detective down inside of me because I see an unsolved case as a personal challenge. I'm not talking about murder cases or robberies, but everyday mysteries, like how the dryer manages to eat only one of my socks every time I use it, leaving me with a dozen mismatched pairs. I'd like to know how my dog always manages to get me to take him for a walk even though I've told him a million times, "No, it's too cold tonight." Mind you, I haven't solved these mysteries yet, but I still ponder them anyway.

There's no mystery when it comes to where my hope lies. There's no mystery to my future or to any believer's future. Our hope and our future are secure in Christ. The mystery that had been kept hidden for ages is that all of us can have salvation through Christ's death. He died for everyone, not just a few.

Yet many people are still trying to figure out the meaning of life, and whether or not there is anything beyond this earthly existence. They hope for whatever they want to achieve. Life here on Earth is everything to them. There can't be any more, they think, because their minds can't absorb the great gift God has given to us, the gift of salvation through Jesus Christ. It's so simple, yet a lot of people miss it. They are still on a quest to solve the mystery of life, to find all of the answers, to be successful, to stay young, and the list goes on.

Colossians 1:27 goes on to say, "To them, God has chosen to make known among the Gentiles the glorious riches of this mystery, which is Christ in you, the hope of glory. The mystery has been revealed. Christ may live in you and you may live forever."

It's that simple. All it takes is for you to believe it and accept it. Then you just place all your hope in Him. Mystery solved.

BUTTONHOLE, BUTTONHOLE, WHO'S GOT THE BUTTONHOLE?

It was starting to turn cold outside so I decided it was time to purchase a new all-weather coat. Robbie Lee, AC, and I went to the nearest mall and started to browse. However, after browsing nearly all day, I still couldn't find a coat to my liking.

"You're just being picky," Robbie Lee said accusingly.

"I just haven't seen anything I like yet, and I'm not buying something I know I won't wear," I shot back.

"Why don't we go and look at flowers?" asked AC. She lives for flowers. No matter what you're in the middle of, AC always suggests looking at flowers as a solution.

"No, I'm not going anywhere else until I find the coat I'm looking for," I said firmly. So the search continued. Finally, in a big department store, I spotted a coat that I liked. It was a gray, double-breasted, all-weather coat.

"Hey, this might do," I said smiling.

"Oh, praise be," gasped Robbie Lee as she fell into a nearby chair placed there for just such occasions.

"Let me try it on because I only see one in my size," I said, walking over to a mirror. Buttoning up the coat however, I noticed right away that there was a button left over, but no buttonhole.

"What's this deal?" I asked walking over to Robbie Lee and AC. "Look, there's this button but no buttonhole for it."

"Let me see that," Robbie Lee said as she examined the coat closely. "You're right."

"Yeah, and I really like this coat too. It's just what I've been looking for," I whined.

"That settles it then. Let's go to Farm Fresh and look at flowers," AC said as she jumped up from her chair.

"No, wait. There's got to be a remedy to this. I'll ask a salesclerk if maybe they can take some money off or perhaps add a buttonhole, because obviously this is a mistake."

After finding a woman arranging clothes on a rack, I walked over, still wearing the prized raincoat I had found.

"Pardon me, but I've tried on this all-weather coat and I really like it, only there appears to be a button here with no buttonhole for it to go into. Is there a way that you can add a buttonhole?" I asked politely.

The salesclerk pondered the situation and examined the coat closely.

"Well I've never seen such a thing," she gasped. "Why would they leave out a buttonhole, you reckon?"

"Well obviously somebody just screwed up," I said convincingly.

"Let me examine these other coats like it," said the salesclerk. She took another coat just like the one I was wearing and put it on. It buttoned up fine with a hole for each of the buttons. "This one seems to be all right."

"Yes, but this one is the only one in my size," I quickly pointed out.

"Hurry up, Polly D. We're getting tired and hungry. We want to stop and get some fried chicken," said Robbie Lee.

"Oh hush, all you ever think about is food. Can't you see I'm in the middle of something here?"

The salesclerk saw an associate manager walking past and called her over. "Margaret, come here, please. Take a look at this."

I boldly stood in front of the associate manager wearing the coat and pointing out that there was a button without a buttonhole. The associate studied the coat and placed her hand on her chin.

"That's very strange," she said. "Did you check the others?"

"Yes, this seems to be the only coat with a missing buttonhole," said the salesclerk.

"I'd really like to buy it, but I'm wondering whether or not you can mend the coat by adding a buttonhole," I said.

"I'm sure that can be arranged," said the associate manager. "Let me look up the costs for such an alteration."

While she was looking through books and catalogs to decide the cost, the salesclerk continued to study the double-breasted, all-weather coat I was still wearing. Suddenly, her face changed colors. She grabbed the coat and began to unbutton it. Then she re-buttoned the coat. Amazingly, now there were an equal number of buttonholes for every button.

"How'd you do that?" I asked with a red face.

"Are you left handed?" asked the salesclerk.

"Well, yes, but I don't see how..."

"You dummy, you buttoned up the double-breasted coat using your left hand and so you buttoned it on the wrong side," Robbie Lee laughed.

The salesclerk and the associate manager just stood with their arms folded glaring at me for taking up so much of their valuable time. I was so embarrassed that I couldn't think of anything to say except, "I'll take it."

As I paid for the coat, Robbie Lee and AC snickered behind my back.

"We could have been eating fried chicken hours ago," said Robbie Lee.

"Yes, and looking at flowers," said AC.

As I walked away with my purchase in a bag, the salesclerk exclaimed in a smug voice, "Let us know if you need assistance in buttoning the coat."

I didn't answer. I just quietly exited the store with Robbie Lee and AC holding each other up as they stumbled into the street with laughter.

"At least I'll be warm," I thought as I quietly vowed never to go back into that store until both the salesclerk and the associate manager were long retired.

MATTHEW 6:3
"But When You Give To The Needy, Do Not Let Your Left Hand Know What Your Right Hand Is Doing."

Isn't it hard to do something nice and not say anything to anyone about it? You just want to tell at least one friend what a wonderful and generous person you are. After all, what's the point in doing something nice for someone if you can't tell the world? Are you just supposed to let it go without saying a word, without receiving any credit? That's exactly right. Otherwise your reward is that brief period of glory. The Bible teaches us to do these good deeds in secret, for the good of the receiver. Our reward will come from the Father, not from anyone here on Earth.

Sometimes we think no one sees the good things we do. We may go without recognition from the world, but the Father sees all that we do. We're His representatives down here. We are to do good because we are striving to be more like Christ, not for any type of immediate reward. If Christ is living in your heart, you'll have a desire to do good and to do the right thing. Now don't misunderstand me, just doing good does not make you a Christian. Accepting Jesus Christ as your personal Savior is the only way you can become a Christian. But after making that decision and allowing Christ to live in your heart, you will find you have a great desire to do things out of love, as our Savior did while He walked on this Earth.

Take the time out of your day to do something good, even if it's a small thing, for someone you don't even know. Watch the expression on their face. You've just been a witness for Christ to that person. Do it without telling others what you've done. Let your reward be in knowing you've just made someone's day a little bit better. Don't let your left hand know what your right hand is doing. Your Father is watching, always.

AFTER-DINNER MINT, ANYONE?

After finishing a meal one evening in one of my favorite restaurants, I decided to pop a breath mint into my mouth since I had been eating onions. I love onions. Everything tastes better with onions. Anyway, right after I had placed the mint in my mouth, I felt the urge to sneeze. Now I don't know about you, but when I sneeze it's usually a whopper. It's not as loud as when Robbie Lee sneezes, however. When she sneezes, people's socks go up and down. I'm talking loud. We had a lovesick moose show up at our door one time after one of Robbie Lee's sneezes. It took several animal control men to come out and move him off our property. I think his heart was broken when he found out it was a human making all that noise.

Anyway, the urge to sneeze just kept getting stronger and stronger. You know, when you've got to sneeze there's nothing that can be done. You just have to let 'er rip. Well, that's what I did. I grabbed my nose and held it shut. That way nothing flies out of it. But this time that move was a big mistake. With my nose tightly held shut, I reared back my head and let it go. The power of the sneeze sent the breath mint in my mouth flying through the air, much to the amazement of me and everyone else at my table. I prayed fervently as I watched it glide through the air in slow-motion, not knowing where it might land.

Splat! It hit a man sitting two tables away right smack dab in the middle of his forehead. He never knew what hit him. I quickly looked away and coaxed my friends at the table to do the same. I didn't want him to even suspect where that flying breath mint originated from. The man unstuck the mint from his forehead and looked at it in disbelief. He glared at everyone all around the restaurant, but no one, except the people at our table, actually saw it hit his head. I stole glances every once in awhile to make sure he wasn't suspicious of anything. I threatened the life of my friends if they so much as smiled.

As we exited the restaurant, I saw the man behind us in line waiting to pay his bill. He didn't look happy. I could just imagine him getting to the front counter, and the cashier asking him if everything was all right.

"The meal was fine," he would probably say. "But I can't say I approve of the way you deliver your after-dinner mints!"

I'll never know for sure. I didn't linger long enough to listen. But all is not lost. At least I learned a valuable lesson from this unfortunate incident. If you feel the urge to sneeze, spit out whatever is in your mouth and cover them both with a handkerchief, napkin, or your hand if need be. I'm just thankful I wasn't eating spinach. It could have been very ugly.

REVELATION 3:16
"So, Because You Are Lukewarm—Neither Hot Nor Cold—I Am About To Spit You Out Of My Mouth."

What kind of Christian are you? I don't mean what denomination. I'm talking about spiritually. Do you do only what you think would be the least expected to get by? Are you only hoping to get into heaven by the skin of your teeth, or are you out to get everything God has for you? Are you constantly praying for God to expand you spiritually so that you can experience everything He has for you?

I once heard someone say that being indifferent is worse than hating something. Being indifferent means you show no interest at all. It means mediocre or lukewarm. I love hot tea and I love ice-cold tea, but lukewarm tea is useless. A hot drink can serve a purpose on a cold day, and a cold drink can be refreshing on a hot and humid day. God is telling us to have some purpose. Don't be halfhearted about something. Being mediocre in your walk will not serve yourself or anyone else any useful purpose. Believe me, making someone spew isn't a pretty sight.

DRIVING WHILE BLIND

One fine sunny Saturday afternoon, Robbie Lee and I were driving home from a long, successful day of shopping.

"Isn't it just lovely today?" I sighed.

"Oh, yes. It's a beautiful day for a cookout. Let's grill some chicken when we get home," said Robbie Lee, smacking her lips.

"Is that all you ever think about? Look around you. It's a gorgeous day, and the birds are singing. I could ride for miles on a day like today."

I rolled down my window and took a long breath of fresh air.

"Of course I can see it's a beautiful day. I'm not blind, just hungry. I think we should have potato salad and baked beans with the chicken," Robbie Lee said, smiling at the thought of such a scrumptious meal.

"I'll make my famous coleslaw," I said with pride.

"We don't need coleslaw and potato salad," Robbie Lee said with a sneer. "Besides, coleslaw is too messy to make. We'll be picking cabbage off the floor for the next six months if you make it."

"I like coleslaw, and I don't make a mess when I fix it," I growled back. "What's grilled chicken without coleslaw?" There was a long period of silence.

"Now see," I said, frowning. "You've got me in a bad mood now."

"Maybe some music will help," said Robbie Lee, turning on the radio. One of our favorite songs came blasting across the airwaves, and I started smiling and singing. We turned it up as loud as it would go and the two of us could be heard singing for miles.

We hadn't noticed that the road we were on had a 25 mph speed limit, and Robbie Lee was going about 40. We were too busy singing the oldies along with the radio to take notice. Suddenly there was a slight break between songs, and I could hear a police siren behind us. As I turned to look, there was a patrol car with its lights flashing and siren blaring right behind us.

"Oh my goodness!" I exclaimed. "It's a policeman. You're speeding! Quick, slow down and pull over. I wonder how long he's been following us."

I put my hand to my head because I felt a big headache coming on. Robbie Lee pulled the car over to the side of the road, and we waited for the policeman to get out of his car.

"Oh, no! I don't have on my glasses," Robbie Lee said searching through her purse. "I must have left them at home. He'll really be upset when he finds out I'm driving around without my glasses."

"How can you drive without your glasses? Your driver's license will tell him you have restricted vision," I said, beginning to panic.

"Well, I guess there's nothing I can do about it now except face the music," Robbie Lee said, sinking into her seat.

"Hey, wait a minute," I said, reaching down between the two seats and fishing around for something.

"You're not looking for a gun, are you?" Robbie Lee asked nervously. "I mean not having my glasses is one thing, but a gun in the car is a whole other problem."

"No, I'm not looking for a gun, although if I had one I would come closer to using it on you right now than the policeman," I said as I kept fishing around between the seats. "Here they are. I knew I had seen an old pair of glasses in the car. Put these on, and he'll never know the difference."

Robbie Lee quickly plopped the glasses on her face and suddenly she was blind. The glasses were covered with dried coca cola, dog hair, tiny pieces of paper and lint.

"I can't see anything with these glasses. If he takes one look, he'll know that I could never drive with these," Robbie Lee turned and looked in my general direction, not actually able to see me. The glasses did look awful, but the policeman was approaching the car so it was too late to do anything about it now.

"Just look straight ahead and listen to everything he says," I whispered.

By the time the police officer reached the car, we could tell that he was really mad.

"Do you ladies know why I stopped you?" he asked, leaning into the window.

"Why no, officer, did we do something wrong?" I innocently responded.

"Wrong? I clocked you going forty miles an hour in a twenty-five mile-an-hour speed zone. That's what you did wrong. Didn't you hear my siren? I've been following you for a couple of miles blasting it as loud as I could."

The policeman looked really angry now.

"Oh, I guess we didn't hear you. We had the radio on a little louder than we should have, I suppose. They were playing some of our favorite songs, and we just started singing and—"

"Don't you know it's dangerous to be driving around with your radio so loud that you can't hear anything? What if an ambulance was behind you, or a fire truck!" The policeman was yelling now.

"You know, he's got a point," Robbie Lee started, but I punched her in the side, so she decided not to finish.

The policeman went on to explain to us that he was going to write out a ticket, and how we could pay it, etc. However, Robbie Lee looked so funny behind the steering wheel, with her head turning in odd directions, trying to pretend she could see. I couldn't help it, but I started to laugh under my breath and that got Robbie Lee started.

"What's so funny? Do you think this is some kind of game?" the policeman snapped.

"No sir. Not at all," Robbie Lee said, trying to keep a straight face. But it was no use. Every time the policeman would start talking, we would crack up laughing. It was one of those times when you're not supposed to laugh, but that makes it worse and so you laugh even harder. Each time he heard us laughing, he would start his speech all over again.

I thought I would die before he finally finished. I was so afraid he was going to ask us to get out of the car and walk a straight line, and with the glasses that Robbie Lee was wearing, I knew that wouldn't be possible.

After writing up the ticket, the policeman stuck it under Robbie Lee's nose and said, "Sign here ma'am."

Robbie Lee just sat there because she wasn't able to see an elephant, more or less where to sign her name. The policeman was beginning to look at Robbie Lee suspiciously, so I cautiously guided Robbie Lee's hand up to the ticket by discreetly taking hold of her elbow. Robbie Lee started signing her name, not even having a clue where she was writing.

Afterwards, the officer stuck a copy of the ticket right in Robbie Lee's face, but I grabbed it before he figured out that she was blind as a bat. He scratched his head, but finally left and returned to his car.

"I didn't think he would ever go," I said, breathing a sigh of relief. We both sat quietly while he drove around us, tipping his hat as he passed by.

"Let's just go home," I said, fanning myself with the ticket.

Robbie Lee started the car and headed home. But she was driving on the shoulder of the road. I looked over to see that she was still wearing the sticky glasses.

"Are you crazy? You can't drive with those glasses on!" I screamed, snatching them off of her face.

"Oh, I must have forgotten I had them on. I guess I was getting used to them. They grow on you after awhile." Robbie Lee pulled back on the road and drove safely the rest of the way home without further incident.

While Robbie Lee sang grossly out of tune to the songs on the radio, I just hung my head out of the window trying to get air.

MATTHEW 15:14
"Leave Them, They Are Blind Guides. If A Blind Man Leads A Blind Man, Both Will Fall Into A Pit."

Have you ever heard someone say that they couldn't be a Christian because they wouldn't be able to follow all the rules? That's what a Christian is to some people, someone who has to follow a bunch of rules just for the sake of following them. Unfortunately, there are religious organizations that do nothing but make sure people are keeping all of their rules instead of teaching them about the love, grace, and mercy of Jesus Christ. They hammer people with rules until they just give up on any hope of following the Christian faith. Their image of God winds up being that of an ogre sitting up in heaven laughing at us because we failed. But that's not how God is at all. He loves us. He loved us so much that he gave His only Son to die for us. Not so we could stumble over man-made rules, but just because He loves us.

The commands and precepts in the Bible are not placed there to keep good, fun things from us. They are there to give us the best we can have for our lives. Christ came so that we might have life, and have it more abundantly. Does that sound like someone who wants us to follow a bunch of empty rules for no reason other than just to prove we can do it? He wants us to live life to its fullest.

Don't be led by the blind. I'm talking about those who can't see God's grace and love and won't allow others to see it, because they are too busy reading you their rules. God is love. He wants you to succeed in the end. He's not putting obstacles in your way to keep you out of Heaven. He loves you so much that He wants to have a very personal relationship with you. Spend time with Him. Get to know Him. Let Him open your eyes to what you can be in Him.

THE CRIPPLE SHALL WALK
(AND FLY)

I was in a cast after having some corrective surgery done on my left foot. It seems that my big toe had somehow decided to hide underneath all the rest of my toes, causing a lot of pain, not to mention lots of stares from strangers when I went barefoot in the summer. My big toe had been this way all of my life, but to others it was a novel sight. After the surgery I took it upon myself to borrow some crutches from a friend rather than wait for the doctor to give me a pair. I didn't bother to make sure the crutches fit my height. After using them for only a couple of days, I developed an enormous pain in my shoulders to the point where I could no longer use the crutches. At this stage I could barely lift a glass of water because the pain was so great. I found myself having to rent a wheelchair to get around town.

Upon renting a wheelchair, I didn't bother asking a lot of questions about its use, figuring there couldn't be a lot to know. After all, I had seen plenty of folks riding in and pushing wheelchairs, so I felt pretty competent I knew most of what there was to know about the subject. Robbie Lee ended up being the one who would have to push me around, but she felt it was the least that she could do for me, the poor soul.

One Sunday morning, I decided I wanted to attend church. This would be my first outing in the wheelchair. Robbie Lee, AC, and I all got dressed up, and when we were all ready, I announced how the wheelchair saga should be handled.

"Robbie Lee, you have the wheelchair waiting in the front yard, and then you help me down the front steps by letting me lean on you with my arm around your neck. That way I can keep the weight off of my foot. Once we reach the bottom of the steps, you'll put the wheelchair up behind me, and I'll sit down. You'll then push me to the car and help me inside. Then you can fold up the wheelchair and place it neatly in the trunk of your car."

"Sounds easy enough," sighed the naive Robbie Lee.

"What should I do?" asked AC.

"You can carry my Bible until I get into the car," I cleverly replied.

So the plan was in place. Without any further instruction, we started on our way to church. First AC went out carrying my Bible and stood patiently waiting at the bottom of the steps. Then Robbie Lee and I followed. I balanced on one foot, holding onto Robbie Lee while the front door was locked and secured. Then I strategically placed my left arm around Robbie Lee's neck and we confidently started down the steps.

The first step went fine, but something happened on the second step. Though we have argued over the years whose fault it was, one of us lost our balance and we quickly came tumbling down the steps, ending up sprawled on the sidewalk below. With our dresses up over our heads and legs in twisted positions, we laid like slugs on the ground.

"Lord, have mercy!" exclaimed AC, with her hand over her mouth. "Get up before the neighbors see you both lying there with your Sunday clothes on all in a heap."

AC was always thinking of what was best for me and Robbie Lee. After all, she had a social position in the community to think about.

With a lot of moaning and groaning and more unladylike maneuvering, we managed to get back up to a standing position.

"Why'd you let me fall?" I naturally asked, while brushing the leaves and twigs from my coat.

"Me?" Robbie Lee said as she spit dirt out of her mouth and tried desperately to stop the three runs that were now in her pantyhose. "I didn't let you fall. You lost your balance. After all, you're the one with only one leg here."

"I was holding onto you. So you must have been the one to fall, sending me crashing to the ground with you like a ton of lard," I accused. "You'll have to be more careful and pay attention to what you're doing from now on."

Robbie Lee decided not to argue anymore as we were already late for church. Falling is always a great waste of time. She grabbed the wheelchair, shoved it behind me, and pulled me backwards into the chair.

"Sit down," she commanded. Robbie Lee pushed the wheelchair down the sidewalk and up to the car. After helping me inside, she began the task of folding up the wheelchair and putting it in the trunk. However, this was not as easy as it looked. After fighting with the chair for awhile she discovered she would have to take off the foot rests in order to get it to fold down.

Robbie Lee had a small yellow Chevrolet Geo with a hatchback. Upon lifting the heavy wheelchair up as high as she could, she found it wouldn't fit. She turned it in every direction she could, trying to force it to fit in the back of the car. Meanwhile, AC and I sat quietly in the car and were subjected to all kinds of exclamations coming from Robbie Lee. Finally the wheelchair fell into place, Robbie Lee slammed down the trunk, and we were off.

Upon arriving at the church, Robbie Lee pulled up to the front so she could get me inside quickly and go park the car. We were terribly late by now, so the three of us were scurrying around like crazy. Robbie Lee didn't even bother turning off the car. After wrestling with the wheelchair for awhile, she managed to get it out of the trunk. Replacing the foot rests, she pushed it up to the car door so I could get in for the ride up to the church. AC still had the job of carrying my Bible until we were well inside the church and seated. She went ahead again, waiting patiently for us to get settled.

Once I was seated in the chair, Robbie Lee took off across the parking lot at breakneck speed, knowing that she still had to park the car. As we were flying toward the church, I was occupied with fixing my hair, which had gotten out of place during the previous fall. I had both hands on my head rather than grasping the arms of the wheelchair, confident in knowing that we had finally arrived at our destination. Robbie Lee spied a dip in the curb made especially for wheelchairs and she headed for it with great speed and vigor.

Now no one had informed us that the best way to approach these ramps is by turning the wheelchair around and backing over it, letting the big wheels of the wheelchair go first. No, Robbie Lee just flew along in the breeze heading for the church. She pushed faster and faster. I was still using both hands to fix my hopeless hair.

Suddenly we hit the small bump in the curve and the wheelchair stopped dead, but I kept on going. Through the air I flew, like a big awkward bird with a broken foot.

"Aaaaaaah!" I screamed as I soared like I had just been shot out of a cannon. Then, once again, I found myself sprawled on the ground with my dress up over my head, right there in front of God, the church, and curious onlookers.

"Lord, have mercy!" exclaimed AC, still holding my Bible.

As I lay on the ground in shock, wondering whether or not I had broken my already broken foot or maybe even my good foot, I could hear these comforting words from Robbie Lee.

"You'll just have to start staying home! That's all there is to it. It's too hard to cart your big behind everywhere in this wheelchair."

"Would someone please help me up?" I asked, trying discreetly to pull my dress back down.

Robbie Lee, who was still standing behind the empty wheelchair, blinked a couple of times, and then ran over and helped me back into the chair. She quickly resumed our journey to the church.

Once inside, she managed to help me to my seat, loudly dropping the wheelchair somewhere at the end of the row. My hair was standing straight up on the top of my head, but I was too dizzy to notice. I barely remember AC handing me my Bible that she had safely carried all the way from the house. I hoped my eyes would stop bouncing by the time it came to the Scripture reading.

When Robbie Lee went back outside to park the car, which was still running, she reached for the door handle only to find that it was locked. She frantically ran around to the other side, but it was locked as well. As tears filled her eyes, she put her head down on the car and wished she had stayed at home. After getting some assistance, she managed to get the car unlocked and parked.

By the time Robbie Lee got to her seat, the singing had already begun. As the rest of the congregation stood smiling and singing, Robbie Lee and I just stood and exchanged dirty looks. However, AC joined the heavenly choir singing loudly and grinning from ear to ear. She had completed her part of the assignment without any problems and was proud to have completed her mission.

MARK 9:45

"And If Your Foot Causes You To Sin, Cut It Off. It Is Better For You To Enter Life Crippled, Than To Have Two Feet And Be Thrown Into Hell."

Is God suggesting we cut off our foot in order to make it into Heaven? No, but He is telling us there are things in our life that we need to cut out if they are keeping us away from spiritual growth. If there are things in your life that you are trying to hold onto, and you know they are wrong, it is better for you to cut them loose, rather than risk jeopardizing your relationship with God. It could be gambling, sexual sin, addiction, or even gossip that you insist on keeping a part of your life because it brings you pleasure or because you don't believe you can live without it. God is saying get rid of it. Don't risk your eternal destination for the temporary pleasure of sin here on Earth.

Ask God for help. That's where prayer comes in. When you feel the temptation rising up inside of you, ask God to give you the strength to overcome it. He's not asking you to do this alone. The Holy Spirit can give you the power you need to beat those things that are keeping you down. If you make a mistake, ask for forgiveness, but don't give up. Don't let the Enemy tell you that you can't make it. With Christ, all things are possible.

ITSY-BITSY SPIDER

Some years back I went camping with some friends in the beautiful setting of the Blue Ridge Mountains. The whole experience was exhilarating. There we were by a rushing mountain stream with a roaring fire, a bag of marshmallows for roasting, some good stories, and good friends. I remember thinking, *why haven't I gone camping more often?*

Then nightfall came. The temperatures dropped to a cool thirty degrees, and I looked forward to sinking into my cozy sleeping bag and zipping it up over my head for the night, dreaming of the next day's adventures. My friends decided to walk up the short trail to the campground facilities to take a hot shower, leaving me with the tent all to myself. I had decided that to really enjoy the camping experience, I would skip the shower and just wear the day's grime to bed. It seemed more realistic somehow. Showering could be done at home and only served to take away from the overall camping smell I had worked so hard to obtain. There was the smell of the smoke from the fire in my clothes and the smell of the well-deserved perspiration from the earlier hike up to Crabtree Falls. I wasn't about to wash away all of these camping merit badges.

So I bid them goodnight and disappeared into the tent with my trusty battery-operated camping lamp. While my friends were up enjoying their sissy hot showers, I was bedding myself down in my warm, snug sleeping bag. I left the lamp on so my friends could easily find their way back to the tent. As I slipped into my bag, I remember feeling proud of myself for being brave enough to wait alone in the tent. As I began to relax, I could hear the stream hurrying past all of the smooth rocks piled in its path. There was a slight breeze causing the trees to creak and sway, but I wasn't afraid. It was a glorious night, and I was safe and warm in my sleeping bag.

As my eyes studied the inside of the tent, I suddenly noticed some movement. It was a shadow, perhaps from the trees, but wait, the shadow was growing. It seemed to cover the entire tent. Were those branches? I rubbed my eyes so I could focus better. When I stopped blinking, I could make out a shape. There was what looked like a spiked circle at the top of the tent with six, no eight squiggly lines extending from its center. What in the world could it be?

As my brain raced through all of its files to match the shape on the tent to an identifiable object, my heart found the answer first, *A spider! It's a spider! A giant spider! Aaaah!* I started kicking and screaming. I was trapped in my stupid sleeping bag in a stupid tent surrounded by a giant, woman-eating spider. I finally managed to rip the zipper down on the bag enough to push myself out of the small opening. It must have looked like a slug giving birth to a full-grown woman flailing around like a fish out of water. I threw everything I could get my hands on at the giant monster, trying to divert its attention while I escaped out of the tent into the night air. As I tumbled out of the tent, I ran right into the startled faces of my friends.

"Run! Run for your lives. What are you waiting for? Can't you see it?

My friends stared back at me as though they were watching a scene from their favorite horror movie. I frantically ran around looking for a huge rock or a piece of wood to fling at the creature. I was willing to risk my life for my friends because they apparently were in a state of shock and unable to defend themselves.

Finally, my friend Jan grabbed me and shook me so hard I suffered whiplash for a month.

"What is wrong with you? Why are you screaming and throwing things? What happened?" she asked. As I looked into her eyes, I could see she was more terrified of me than of the huge creature sitting in our tent.

"It's a giant spider, can't you see it?" I asked, frantically pointing at the tent. But as I looked, I could see there was nothing there. It had gone as quickly as it had appeared. There was silence. All eyes were on me.

"Watch her," Jan said. "I'll check out the tent."

While the others stood guard over me and glared at me like I was an escapee from a mental ward, Jan opened the flap of the tent, laughing at the top of her lungs.

"Is this what you saw?" she asked, holding up the lamp to reveal a small, frail, frightened spider trying desperately to climb out of the back of the tent. "He probably walked near your lamp and it made a giant shadow on the tent," said Jan.

Poor guy, he looked as scared as I felt. He was only looking for a little warmth and a place to sleep, but instead found havoc and mayhem.

As my friends went into the tent, they shook their heads, laughing and recalling over and over again how my face looked as I came flying out of the tent. Jan told me later that their flashlight had broken while they were returning from the showers, but they had no trouble finding the tent because they just followed my terrifying screams. I was so humiliated.

Eventually the snickers and sarcasm gave way to the snorts and whistles of my friends sleeping. I stayed awake. I was sure the theory about the lamp and the shadow was true, but you just never know. It would be a long night, but exhilarating nonetheless.

PSALM 27:1
"The Lord Is My Light And My Salvation—Whom Shall I Fear? The Lord Is The Stronghold Of My Life—Of Whom Shall I Be Afraid?"

The events of September 11, 2001, left me terrified and shocked. I actually remember thinking to myself that from then on nothing would ever be the same. For the first time, my future felt threatened. I had a hard time seeing beyond the horrible sights of that day. I was glued to my television set like everyone else, trying to make sense of what I had just seen and heard. My fear level was at an all-time high. I feared for my country and for my family's safety and security. I suddenly realized how fragile my life was and how vulnerable we all are. I cried out to God for comfort and peace, and I found it in His Word. Psalm 27 asks "Whom shall I fear?" I learned that I could not rely on the world for my well-being, but that I had to place my trust in God to keep me safe and to place my hope for the future in Him. Psalm 27 goes on to say, "Though an army besiege me, my heart will not fear, though war break out against me, even then will I be confident." My fears began to subside.

God's Word reminded me that He was my foundation and that His promises are true. In this world, we will have troubles, but Jesus has conquered the world. We've already won. There is nothing to fear. If He is for us, who can be against us? We face many fears throughout our lives: fear of man, rejection, failure, being alone, etc. Sometimes we allow these fears to shape our lives, our decisions, and our future. Jeremiah 29:11 tells us, "For I know the plans I have for you, declares the Lord, plans to prosper you and not to harm you, plans to give you hope and a future." Don't let fear be the deciding factor in your life. It can paralyze you and take away your dreams. Proverbs 3:5 tell us to "Trust in the Lord with all your heart and lean not on your own understanding." Sometimes we allow even the smallest fears to dictate what we will or will not do, until that small fear turns into the dominating factor around which all our decisions are made. Make a list of your fears and tackle them one by one. Look to God's Word for encouragement and guidance. He has made you the head and not the tail. Don't let the Enemy use fear to control your life and your future. After all, God has made us more than conquerors through His love.

IN CONCLUSION

I hope while reading these stories and Bible Scriptures that you have found your-self remembering your own funny family experiences. I realize not all of the Scriptures cited were inspired and written with just my family adventures in mind, and usually have a much larger implication. But as I stated previously, I believe God has given each of us a sense of humor and with that gift we can choose to see even Biblical Scriptures in a humorous light. The Bible was written to provide us not only with a world vision, but a vision for our own everyday lives.

The sense of humor I've been blessed with has not made me blind to my fam-ily's annoying or embarrassing moments, but I believe it has helped me open my eyes wider and see more than what appears on the surface. I appreciate those moments more than ever as I've gotten older. Both my father and my older brother are deceased now. Instead of remembering the hard and negative side of my life with them, I find myself cherishing the times we had and wishing we had spent more time laughing with and at one another.

Take the time to view your family life with a different set of eyes. Whether it be your mother, father, brothers and sisters, or husband, wife and children, make a conscious choice to allow your vision to include the humorous side of life. Don't allow yourself to believe you're now too old or too mature to laugh. When I choose to laugh at situations I find myself in, it seems I actually get through the harder times more easily. The choice to have humor in my life has added the abil-ity to lighten not only my load, but the load of others around me. It's easy to spread negativity and depression, but spreading humor and laughter takes more strength. It's saying, "I know it's hard sometimes, but get up and keep going. Don't be afraid to laugh out loud at life." Hard times and trials will come, there's no doubt about that. So why not choose to add another dimension to your family life? Stop and take a look around. The funny side of life is there. After you've allowed time for the tears, make a decision to allow twice as much time to laugh. Life is a buffet of choices. So choose not to fill your plate with just heaping help-ings of arguing, crying, disagreements, and bitterness. Leave room on your plate for the lighter side of life. Leave room for the laughter.

978-0-595-36797-9
0-595-36797-6

Printed in the United States
61956LVS00003B/181-183

9 780595 367979